Making
Your Church

MW00333063

A
PLACE
TO
SERVE

Making
Your Church

A
PLACE
TO
SERVE

Involving
Members the
Southeast Way

DON WADDELL

 COLLEGE PRESS PUBLISHING COMPANY
JOPLIN, MISSOURI

Copyright © 2001
College Press Publishing Company
On the web at www.collegepress.com
Toll-free order line 1-800-289-3300

Printed and Bound in the
United States of America
All Rights Reserved

Cover Design by Brett Lyerla

Library of Congress Cataloging-in-Publication Data

Waddell, Don, 1945–
    Making your church a place to serve: involving
members the Southeast way/Don Waddell.
        p.   cm.
    Includes bibliographical references.
    ISBN 0-89900-870-4 (pbk.)
    1. Church membership.   2. Church growth.
3. Church work.   4. Southeast Christian Church
(Louisville, Ky.)   I. Title.
BV820.W23 2001
253—dc21
                                            00-065927

Table of Contents

Introduction

On July 1, 1962, I was one of 53 former South Louisville Christian Church members who responded to the invitation and transferred our family's membership to a brand new church called Southeast Christian Church. From that inauspicious beginning, God began a work that would grow in 38 years to a megachurch where 14,000 to 15,000 worship each weekend. While the overall worship attendance has been more noticeable, a less apparent phenomenon has contributed significantly to our growth. From the very beginning, Southeast has been a church where a large percentage of the congregation is actively involved in the ministry of the church.

The purpose of this book is to explain our program for leading people to Christ and to membership at Southeast and then for more fully involving those members in the work God is doing in the Louisville area and "to the uttermost ends of the earth." I hope to provide the reader a practical, how-to description of an effective new member assimilation process that begins when a guest drives onto the campus or walks into the church for the first time and continues through membership and greater levels of involvement.

I want to emphasize from the beginning that we don't have all the answers. Like many of you, we're still struggling and experimenting. We are routinely trying new programs, saving the ones that work and discarding the others. In the pages that follow, I will describe where we are today, knowing that it will begin to change before the ink is dry on the paper. Nevertheless, I believe what we have developed is a sound, effective program that can help you as you seek to assimilate new members and more fully involve your existing membership.

Let me say a word on how to use the material in this book and accompanying Internet downloads available at *www.collegepress.com*. Though copyrighted, Southeast Christian Church hereby grants a revocable, nonexclusive, nonprofit license for churches of all denominations to copy any item containing the Southeast Christian Church copyright notice (both the electronic appendixes on the web page and the charts in the printed book) for use in their local ministries, provided that (i) such church receives no remuneration for such copies, other than the reasonable cost of reproduction, and (ii) all copies include the Southeast Christian Church copyright notice as printed on the item. However, this license does not extend to any part of this work that has been reprinted or otherwise included with the permission of another author. Requests for permission to reprint portions of the text of this book should be addressed to the publisher, College Press Publishing Co.

This book would not have been possible without the unselfish efforts of Les Hughes, my good friend and coworker for Jesus Christ. He served as a primary contributor since his involvement in Southeast's New Member program predates mine by years. He has provided major portions of the material from his experience, and I appreciate his efforts. I would also like to express my appreciation to fellow coworkers in Southeast's New Member ministry. Their names are: Esther Jaggers, Susie Carter, Kay Sue Leppert, and Kindra

McComas. These ladies are tireless, devoted servants of our Savior. Without their dedication to Southeast and Jesus, our program would have been far less effective and this book would not have been possible. In addition, I have received enormous support from deacons who are part of the New Member ministry and key leaders as well as literally hundreds of volunteers. Finally, I thank God for my devoted wife, Nancy, who has provided behind-the-scenes support, wise counseling, proofreading, and encouragement during the arduous and time-consuming process of writing a book.

Part One

FIRST, A LITTLE BACKGROUND IS IN ORDER

Chapter 1

Southeast History: From Church Plant to Megachurch

*Then the church throughout Judea, Galilee and Samaria enjoyed
a time of peace. It was strengthened; and encouraged by the
Holy Spirit, it grew in numbers, living in the fear of the Lord.*

Acts 9:31

Before launching into a discussion of the specifics of our
program, I'd like to briefly review the history of Southeast Christian Church. I do this because many of the important assimilation principles upon which we have built our
program were introduced long ago but not formalized into a
new member assimilation program until recently.

South Louisville Christian Church started Southeast in
1962 as the most recent of three previous church plants.
The new congregation met in a local elementary school cafe-
teria for several months before purchasing a house that
would become the church building for several years. Plans
for a new building with a 550-seat sanctuary were drawn up
in 1963 and in 1967 the new facility was dedicated. **It is significant that the original building was constructed so that its
sanctuary could not be enlarged.** The rationale for this decision
was that when the church outgrew the sanctuary, it would
start another church just as South Louisville had started
Southeast.

As a recent Cincinnati Bible College graduate, Bob Russell joined the church in 1966 and has remained with Southeast to this day. In his book *High Expectations*, Thom Rainer found that one of the factors consistently associated with the most "effective" churches was a long tenure of its senior pastor.[1] In this respect, Southeast has been richly blessed.

Southeast continued to expand and modify its facility over the next 11 years. The first additional staff member, a youth minister, was hired in 1973. A second service was added in 1975 after having been previously rejected by the membership. As the congregation grew, a third service was added in 1980 and a fourth in 1984, the same year ground was broken for a new building, which was to be built a half mile from the original church. A children's staff person was also added in 1984.

Obviously, relocating to a new building as opposed to starting a new church was a significant change from the earlier intention to start another church when the congregation outgrew its facility. I believe this change was the most significant decision ever made by Southeast's leadership. In retrospect it appears to have been a wise decision based on considerable prayer and a prescient awareness of the changing culture in America.

An expanding Interstate system and greater reliance on the automobile made it possible for Americans to become more mobile. In addition the growing suburbs tended to de-emphasize community-based activities. In contrast to earlier times, Americans in the 1980s were more inclined to get in their cars and travel where their needs could be best met rather than limiting themselves to local stores, communities, and churches. As a consequence, **the community church began to give way to larger churches.**

At about the same time, Americans began to disassociate themselves from mainline denominations and independent, nondenominational churches began to grow and prosper. Thus began the megachurch movement. According to the April 1, 1999, *USA Today* more than 1.7 million U.S. Protestants now attend "megachurches" (2,000-plus attendees per week), and the number of megachurches has grown from just 10 in 1970 to 470 in 1998.[2] As reported in the *Los Angeles Times*, July 17, 1999, edition, an average of one church joined the above-1,000 ranks every three days in 1998.[3] Had Southeast's leadership not abandoned its earlier church plant paradigm, the results would have been altogether different.

In 1976, the Living Word tape ministry began. This became an important program that would pay enormous dividends for the church. Due to increasing demand for copies of his sermons, a member began taping Bob's messages using a jury-rigged laptop recorder and cheap microphone. Demand continued to increase until the church formalized the program and began to sell larger numbers of tapes each week. Eventually in 1981, the church would buy time on a local radio station to air Bob's messages.

In 1987, the congregation moved into its new, 127,000 square foot facility containing a sanctuary that could seat 2,200 people. However, despite much prayer and negotiation, we were unable to sell the old church building. Though many of us were concerned over our inability to sell the building, it was to later become a blessing. After we occupied our new facility, worship attendance grew by 40% the first year, and soon the old building was pressed into action as a youth complex. A third service was added in 1988, and three years later 88 acres of land were purchased eight miles from the old buildings for a new church with a sanctuary that would seat over 8500. We occupied our new, 770,000-square-foot facility in December 1998.

The chart below depicts the worship attendance, Bible School growth, and membership additions from 1962 until 1998. You can see the church sustained excellent growth of approximately 10% until we moved into our new building in 1987 when worship attendance increased 40% in a year and continued its impressive growth into the 1990s. Bible School attendance also grew, but at a lesser rate. The number of people joining the church increased from a hundred or so per year to over 1,700 in 1998 and 2,457 in 1999.

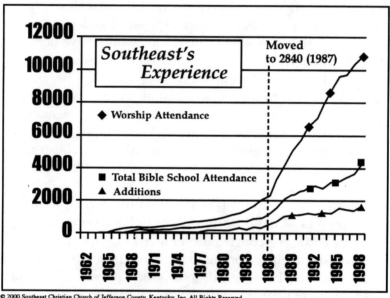

© 2000 Southeast Christian Church of Jefferson County, Kentucky, Inc. All Rights Reserved

Chart 1: Southeast's Growth Since 1962

Southeast's leadership would be quick to give God the credit for the exceptional growth we have achieved and acknowledge that much remains to be done. What are the factors that have led to this profound success? In the pages that follow, I intend to enumerate some of those factors.

Chapter 2

Secrets of Southeast's Success:
A Layman's Perspective

Therefore, take care to follow the commands, decrees and laws I give you today. If you pay attention to these laws and are careful to follow them, then the LORD your God will keep his covenant of love with you, as he swore to your forefathers. He will love you and bless you and increase your numbers.

Deuteronomy 7:11-13

Bob Russell has written a book published with Howard Publishing entitled *When God Builds a Church*. In it he outlines some factors that led to Southeast's success and are essential for any church to flourish over time. The list that follows parallels Bob's thinking but takes a slightly different perspective. My perspective is that of a charter member more than casually involved as a young adult in the formative years of the church. However, because I entered the military in 1967, I was away from the church for 28 years.

During this time, I benefited in three ways: *One*, I kept up with Southeast through my parents and by listening to Bob's sermon tapes religiously, so to speak. I also visited Southeast several times a year and maintained close contact with the church. *Two*, I was blessed by serving in leadership capacities in many other churches as my wife and I moved to different duty locations during my Air Force career. This allowed me to compare and contrast Southeast's experience with that of other churches of varying sizes. *Three*, over the course of my military career I was steeped in leadership training and taught leadership and management at Air War College, a post graduate school for senior officers in the Department of Defense. For these reasons, I bring a slightly different perspective to Southeast's evolution than some closer to the action.

In my opinion, there are ten leadership practices, programs, and principles Southeast has employed to achieve its extraordinary success over the past 38 years.

TEN REASONS FOR SUCCESS

1. **Southeast has set and, for the most part, achieved a number of BHAGs, or Big Hairy Audacious Goals.** In his book, *Built to Last*, Jim Collins asserted that successful, visionary organizations set their sights high and pursue goals lesser organizations are afraid to attempt. He called them "BHAGs."[4] **Bob Russell has repeatedly challenged us to "attempt something so impossible that it would fail if God's not in it."** That's a BHAG by another name. Certainly our building programs were BHAGs. As an indicator of how forward looking and faithful our leadership was, plans for the building we currently occupy were begun after we had been in our old building only two years. The associated capital campaigns also required the church leadership and congregation to step out on faith.

In 1995, the church tackled another BHAG and decided to begin publishing a weekly newspaper. Since we were in the middle of a significant building program and publishing a newspaper was out of a church's normal area of expertise, many didn't hold out much hope for a successful outcome. Four years later the paper is self-supporting and has expanded to three sections, becoming one of the largest newspapers in the state.

2. **Southeast and its leadership have not been discouraged by closed doors.** Early in the church's history our first minister resigned, and the search for a replacement took longer than we expected. One of our elders came in contact with Bob Russell about the time he graduated from seminary. We offered him the job, but he declined having already committed to another church for a year. Undeterred by this apparent closed door, the elders waited, and a year later Bob accepted a position at Southeast.

I can also recall being concerned that our neighbor next to the original church building wouldn't sell his house to allow us room to expand. I just knew that would interfere with our growth plans. Our inability to buy this property was one of the factors that prompted us to build a new facility instead of expanding at our former location. Then I worried when we were unable to sell our old building. Our leaders weren't overly concerned, and, in the end, we made great use of the old building as our Youth Complex.

3. **The staff is fully empowered and decentralized.** We have hired highly qualified ministers and support staff personnel, given them a vision for their ministry, and then let them go. Neither Bob nor the elders felt the need to be involved in every aspect of the operation, thus allowing the ministries the autonomy they needed to grow and prosper. I have seen many churches stumble because the senior minister wanted to maintain a tight grip on everything that happened. Secular organizations often succumb to the same temptation to micromanage.

Southeast attained an unusual balance of control and empowerment. In their book, *In Search of Excellence*, Tom Peters and Robert Waterman identify this as one of their eight basic principles of successful companies and call it "Simultaneous Loose-Tight Properties." They write: "It (the eighth principle) is in essence the co-existence of firm central direction and maximum individual autonomy. . . . Organizations that live by the loose-tight principle are on the one hand rigidly controlled, yet at the same time allow (indeed, insist on) autonomy, entrepreneurship, and innovation from the rank and file." [5]

4. **The church leadership committed us to standards of excellence in everything we do.** In church business, it's easy to compromise on quality, but Southeast has been steadfastly committed to the highest standards of excellence in everything we do. Those standards of professionalism are particularly obvious during our worship services. But they are also apparent in every aspect of our operation from the condition of the facility, the friendliness of our greeters, the cleanliness of our restrooms, or the operation of the parking lot to the fact that every service begins on time. This is important to those of us in the assimilation business because it plays a role in visitors returning and new members wanting to get involved. People are naturally attracted to an activity that is done well. The reverse is also true: They are reluctant to commit to programs that are done in a slipshod manner.

It has been said that a visitor will make a decision whether or not to return to a church during the first 4-7 minutes. That means that the first impression a visitor gets begins at the front gate, parking lot, and lobby, not just the worship service and other programs. If that impression is based on quality, professionalism, and excellence, the visitor is more likely to return.

5. **The staff has been willing to change.** I don't know what it is about Christians, but often we seem absolutely terrified of change. Yet the reality is that organizations unwilling to change, those that are reluctant to adapt their way of doing business, decline and die. Tom Peters chronicles the practices of 43 "excellent" companies such as IBM, Caterpillar, and others and reduced his findings to eight principles these companies practiced. The implication was obvious. Adopt these principles in your firm and you, too, can excel. Several years later, however, Peters noticed that many of the 43 companies had declined appreciably. He later wrote *Thriving*

on Chaos in which he attributed the fall of the formerly successful companies to the fact that they had continued to do things the way that had brought success in the past while their competitors were adopting new and more efficient ways of doing business. He concluded "we must learn to love change as much as we have hated it in the past."[6]

Southeast has demonstrated a willingness to change. Bob has expressed this as our "being willing to change methods, but not the message." As a consequence, our services and programs appeal to a broad cross-section of seekers and long-time Christians. While there are literally hundreds of significant changes in the church's history, three stand out as most significant. Some may not sound too revolutionary now, but at the time they encountered stiff opposition from segments of the congregation who wanted to continue to do business the way that had brought success in the past.

The first significant change occurred in 1966 when a group of elders from the "Builders" generation hired a 22-year-old, virtual "Baby Boomer" as their senior minister. This was a big change representing a significant break with the past. Second, as noted earlier, I believe the most profound change in our history occurred when the church's leadership decided to build a larger building rather than begin a new church as originally intended.

Third, the next most significant change was the addition of a Saturday service in the early 1990s. As you can imagine, this proposal generated a good deal of controversy. While other faiths routinely worship on Saturday, the independent Christian churches had not since we seek to pattern our church after the first-century model as much as possible. The early church met on the "first day of the week." Bob has always counseled "in matters of doctrine unity, in matters of opinion liberty, in all things love." However, after much prayer and Bible study, we decided that when you worship God is a matter of opinion and not doctrine. Unfortunately, some traditionalists are still searching for the scripture that says: "Thou shalt not worship the LORD thy God at any time other than Sunday morning."

The point can be made here that the reason we went to a Saturday service was to make more room available on Sunday, the services most visitors attended. The long-standing members of our congregation were encouraged to commit to two years of Saturday night worship. Then, when the new facility was ready all could move back to Sunday morning worship. No one thought the Saturday worship would become the evangelistic outreach it has become, reaching many who would never (or perhaps could not) come on Sunday.

The addition of a Saturday service in the early 1990s was necessitated mostly by overcrowding on Sundays, but it had unintended benefits in other areas. At the time, the quality movement within the U.S. business community was emphasizing consumer needs, offering more options and better customer service. By offering another day to worship, Southeast benefited by allowing "consumers" another opportunity to include church in their increasingly busy schedules.

As a church, Southeast also benefited by now attracting individuals of other faiths who were accustomed to worshiping on Saturday. I need to add at this point: Southeast has never intentionally tried to attract people who were attending other churches. We are first and foremost committed to leading unbelievers and the unchurched to a saving relationship with Jesus Christ. At the same time we realize that much of our growth has come by way of people who transfer their membership from their church to Southeast. Bob defends this circumstance by saying that "we sow grass, we don't steal sheep."

6. *As already mentioned in our Southeast historical recap,* **the tape ministry has been a valuable tool for getting Bob and the gospel out to where people can hear both.** "I first heard about Southeast on the radio during one of Bob's sermons" is the

second most often mentioned response to the question: "What first attracted you to Southeast?" They heard Bob on the radio and decided to come to church to hear more.

7. *While many churches have a mission statement today,* **Southeast was the first church I know who adopted a mission statement and this statement has guided us for many years now.** Not only were we among the first to have a mission statement, but it's a good one presenting the values and purpose of the organization in words that are succinct and memorable. Our mission is to: Evangelize the lost, edify the saved, minister to those in need and be a conscience in the community." For more than a decade this biblically based statement has helped us focus on the purpose of Christ's church and has guided us in the details of achieving that purpose whether it be in preparing the budget, fielding new programs, or determining which articles to publish in our church paper.

8. **The church has taken great pains to hire and retain the right people.** The observation that quality begets quality is particularly true in the area of hiring new employees. Hiring a new employee at Southeast is based on an elaborate, spiritually focused process that emphasizes a person's personal relationship with Jesus Christ first and their qualifications for the job second. Until recently we hired only members, but the new building has required us to ease this policy in the food service and custodial areas. This "members only" policy has served us well by ensuring that the people we hired understood our core values and were acquainted with the Southeast way of doing business.

We have also been willing to wait for God to bring us the people we needed. The increased activity associated with Southeast's phenomenal growth, particularly in the 1990s, created an imperative to hire new people. Nevertheless, despite the temptation to hire the first warm body to submit a résumé, we waited, often for months until the Lord sent us just the right person. This was painful but essential. Overall, this policy of waiting for the right person has resulted in unbelievably low employee turnover and exceptional continuity in our ministries.

9. **Another secret to Southeast's success is that the church is simply a great place to work.** Our people genuinely like each other. We laugh a lot and have a good time while serving the Lord and leading souls to salvation. Katherine Graham, former publisher of the *Washington Post*, commented on how she felt about her job by saying: "To love what you're doing; and believe it makes a difference — what could be better?" If that applies to publishing a newspaper, it is even more rewarding in the context of leading souls to an eternal relationship with God through His Son. I have been associated with some pretty good units in the past such as fighter squadrons and ball teams where the camaraderie was excellent. I believe Southeast's esprit de corps exceeds even the best units (probably because our Esprit is Holy).

10. *Finally, and most importantly for the subject of this book,* **it has been the expectation that church members would be participants and not just spectators.** Everyone pitches in to accomplish the work of the church. Sure, this policy saves money, but more importantly it gets people involved in serving God and being part of the exciting work God is performing here. That was illustrated most recently when we had over 2000 people assist in cleaning the new building before we moved in. It's also apparent in other robust volunteer programs such as hospital visitation, ushers, greeters, parking, children's department, etc. The church has a library providing in excess of 15,000 volumes that was begun and has been sustained largely by volunteers (and my mom). For many years our sanctuary has been cleaned on Monday mornings primarily by volunteers from one Sunday School class. The list could go on.

I credit our church's leaders with establishing this principle from the very beginning and creating an environment where Southeast could grow and flourish through the "living sacrifices" of our members. It was an expectation from the very beginning that we'd use volunteers to accomplish much of the work at the church even though this approach is more difficult than hiring staff to do the work. While the benefits of volunteers are significant in terms of manpower and money saved, relying on volunteers creates a corporate attitude of ownership and participation among the laity. The more people you can involve in the work of the church, the more people you'll have who are fully committed to accomplishing the mission of the church.

But empowering the laity is scriptural as well as practical. As Paul wrote to the church in Ephesus: "It was he who gave some to be apostles, some to be prophets, some to be evangelists, and some to be pastors and teachers, to prepare God's people for works of service, so that the body of Christ may be built up until we all reach unity in the faith and in the knowledge of the Son of God and become mature, attaining to the whole measure of the fullness of Christ" (Ephesians 4:11-13). Our job as ministers and lay leaders is to "prepare God's people." This imperative to involve the laity is embodied in the current church growth paradigm of "The Equipping Church." I believe Southeast has been an equipping church from the very beginning.

While it is impossible to know the mind of God and to determine why some churches are more successful than others, **I'm confident that any church can benefit by applying to their organization the 10 principles, practices, and programs I have observed here at Southeast.** Many of these "secrets" led to the creation of the New Member Ministry, which will be described in the next chapter.

Chapter 3

History of the
New Member Ministry:
It's Uniquely Southeast

*Consider it pure joy, my brothers, whenever you face trials of
many kinds, because you know that the testing of your faith
develops perseverance. Perseverance must finish its work so
that you may be mature and complete, not lacking anything.*
                                                    James 1:2-4

The New Member Ministry at Southeast formally began
in the early 1990s, but the essential assimilation principles were implicitly resident in the church from the very
beginning. As our review of Southeast's history and secrets
to our success revealed, Bob Russell and the early elders
charted a course based on principles of congregational participation, a dedication to excellence, and not being afraid
of change. As the staff grew, new staff members initiated
programs based on the vision, values, and basic principles
that were foundational to the organization. Such was the
case with the New Member program. Making new members
and involving them were clear expectations even before we
hired a minister, Les Hughes, to formalize the program.

Two New Ministries

In 1990 at the recommendation of the Adult Bible Fellowship committee, the church hired two new ministers and initiated two new programs: a small group ministry and a spiritual gifts ministry. It is worth noting that at the time our weekly attendance was "only" 5,500 and both ministries were relatively new to the church growth movement. Les Hughes's challenge was to expand a program that had been developed by an intern. To that end, he visited a number of other churches and attended Leadership Network's first conference on lay mobilization. As the first Spiritual Gifts program was fielded, all elders and deacons took the class. **Getting the church leadership on board at the very beginning was a critically important part of the success of the program that was to follow.** It paid dividends not only in support by the leadership, but it had collateral benefits in recruiting volunteers and building upon the expectation that everyone participated in the work of the church.

Initially, the Spiritual Gifts Class consisted of four one-hour sessions conducted on Sunday evenings. When the church leadership decided to cease Sunday evening worship services in 1992, the program was consolidated into a single four-hour session on Saturday morning. This format has been very successful in attracting the maximum number of people. We tried four, one-hour sessions again in 1999 and eventually canceled that class as attendance dwindled over time.

In his capacity as Spiritual Gifts Minister, Les inherited several other loosely related functions in 1995 such as ushers, communion servers, and greeters. In 1998 his responsibilities changed to focus more time and attention to the New Member Ministries and Decision Counselors and a Guest Services Director was brought on board to oversee the ushers, communion servers, greeters, and related ministries. Les's responsibilities were again expanded in 1998 to include New Member Ministries and Decision Counselors.

Soon, however, it became apparent that we should be doing a better job of keeping up with the rapidly increasing number of new members joining the Church. The New Member ministry was being overwhelmed by sheer numbers as 150-200 people joined the church each month. Moreover, it wasn't clear that new members were getting involved at the same rate as they had in the past. Worse yet, we had no mechanism to determine how well we were doing.

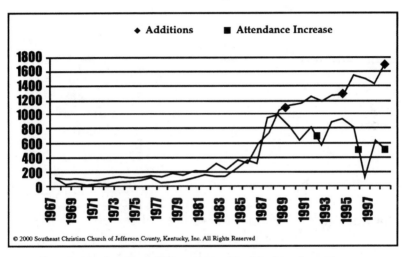

© 2000 Southeast Christian Church of Jefferson County, Kentucky, Inc. All Rights Reserved

Chart 2. Membership Additions versus Worship Attendance Increase

Looking at the chart you can see that up until about 1987, worship attendance increased proportionately to the new members added. However, in 1988, a year after we moved into our second building and people began to join in record numbers, the ratio of worship attendance increase to new members began to decline dramatically. Since 1967 when we began collecting data, worship attendance has increased by 55 for every 100 people who joined. In 1998 we added 1,709 new members while worship attendance increased only 510, or a rate of 30 per 100. Obviously, worship attendance is the minimum level of involvement, and we hope for something more from the majority of people.

Granted there were a number of exacerbating factors that discouraged regular attendance at Southeast. We were cramming more than 10,000 people in five services, our 2200-seat sanctuary was maxed out, and the parking lot was a considerable annoyance. Still, it was clear that we needed an expanded new member program to contend with the massive number of new members the Lord was sending our way.

INVOLVEMENT MINISTRY

For these reasons, another ministerial position was added to focus exclusively on the involvement process, which I will describe later. At the time, I had been working as Director of Facilities since joining the Southeast staff in 1995. But when we moved into our new, more sophisticated building, we brought a plant engineer on board and I was offered the opportunity to become the Involvement Minister and oversee the assimilation of new members after they joined the church. The church leadership felt that we had an effective Decision Counseling process and a sound spiritual gifts program, but we needed someone to oversee the total program of involvement. To this end, Les Hughes's responsibilities were narrowed to getting guests and regular attendees through the decision counseling process and into the baptistery.

My responsibilities began once they emerged from the baptistery. While we worked as a team and there is substantial overlap, particularly in the staff support area, this structure has been a logical, coherent way to move our people from guest to new member to active servant at Southeast. Initially, the New Member Ministry was assigned to the adult education minister. After a year, however, we moved it over to the Director of Ministries. (See organizational Charts 3 and 4.)

In the early years of President Reagan's administration, I worked in the Pentagon in the office that planned for the acquisition of fighter aircraft. The President was committed to bolstering the U.S. military after years of neglect, and money was flowing rapidly into the Pentagon. In our zeal to field new airplanes, however, we were not procuring the requisite support systems to go along with the new equipment. Regrettably, we made the same mistake in the New Member ministry. My position was added without adding another support person to contend with all the additional work I was generating. To compensate for this oversight we added a new support position to coordinate our various programs seven months after I came on board. (See Appendix 30 [downloadable from the internet — see p. 160] for the secretarial job description.)

It took me less than a year to determine that **we needed more help in every aspect of assimilation but were particularly hurting in the area of connecting people to ministry.** While this process will be described in Chapters 7 and 8, I will note here that we added a ministerial assistant position about a year after I moved to New Members. This person focused her energies on identifying the volunteer needs of the ministries and matching those needs with people who were ready to get involved.

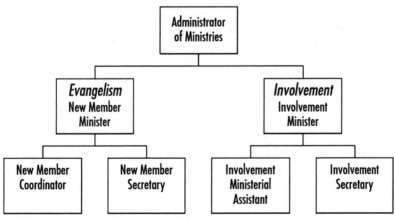

© 2000 Southeast Christian Church of Jefferson County, Kentucky, Inc. All Rights Reserved

Chart 3: New Member Ministry Organization

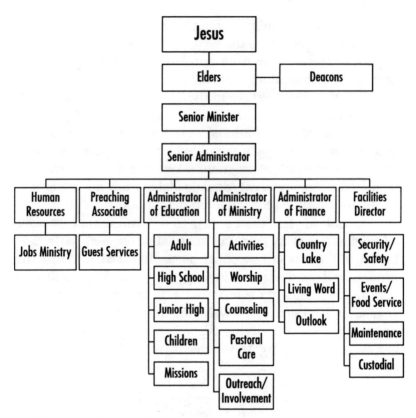

© 2000 Southeast Christian Church of Jefferson County, Kentucky, Inc. All Rights Reserved

Chart 4: Southeast Organization

Chapter 4

A Model for a Model Assimilation Program

And so you became a model to all the believers in Macedonia and Achaia. The Lord's message rang out from you not only in Macedonia and Achaia—your faith in God has become known everywhere.   1 Thessalonians 1:7-8

DEFINITION OF TERMS

I must confess that when I was asked to be Southeast's Involvement Minister and oversee our "assimilation process," I wasn't sure what we were talking about, so I started by looking the word up in the dictionary. I really did. The word "assimilate" is from the Latin meaning "to make similar." Its definition is **1 a**: to take in and appropriate as nourishment: absorb into the system **b**: to take into the mind and thoroughly comprehend **2 a**: to make similar **b**: to alter by assimilation **c**: to absorb into the cultural tradition of a population or group. *Synonym*: absorb. **Clearly the emphasis is on making new members become integral, contributing parts of the congregation, and to absorb them into the church body.**

As we have institutionalized the process, the church community has used a number of other terms such as "lay mobilization" and "involvement." The term currently in vogue is "equipping" and finds its origin in "preparing God's people for works of service," as Paul wrote in Ephesians 4. The thought of equipping the saints has a nice connotation. That is, our job as the pastoral staff isn't to do the work, and to a certain extent it isn't even to delegate church work. Our job is to actually organize, train, and equip the laity, so that as the body of Christ they are equipped, empowered, and provided the resources to do what the Holy Spirit leads us to do.

The above definition of the word "assimilate" and Paul's emphasis on equipping the saints to do the work of the church provides an excellent characterization of the aims and purposes of the New Member ministry at Southeast. These purposes are stated in our ministry mission statement:

Guide seekers to

1) Receive Christ as their personal Lord and Savior;

2) Become members of the Body of Christ at Southeast, finding their spiritual gifts and using those gifts in service to our Lord by ministering to others;

3) Guide new members to a deeper level of spiritual maturity and service.

Recently, I reviewed two videotapes on assimilation programs at 18 megachurches. The specifics of the programs were as varied as the number of churches interviewed. As I read every book on assimilation I could get my hands on and considered the information on the videos, I identified five general assimilation principles. I believe we have been reasonably successful in incorporating these principles into our program.

FIVE GENERAL PRINCIPLES

1. **A successful assimilation program involves the entire congregation.** It's not just a program run by a member of the staff. It can't be another "Program of the Month." Everyone assumes responsibility for getting new members involved, greeting visitors, inviting them to various classes, calling new members, or just being friendly. I listened to Bruce Bugbee at the Leadership Network Conference in San Antonio in 1999 describe how important this principle is. He said that our assimilation process has to become a value to our church and our leadership. In all too many cases, assimilation is introduced as another program, the latest fad to help the church grow. To be effective and to be biblically correct, it must be more. It has to become an integral part of how we do business. According to Bugbee, equipping the saints is like worship, prayer, evangelism, and the other essentials of the church. It must be embraced by all and included as an inseparable part of the giving of our best to the Master.

2. **Personal, authentic contact by a guest or new member with the senior ministry staff is vital.** Afterwards, contact with the community of believers is more important; but initially the guest and new member want to know that the senior ministers are approachable and sincerely interested in their welfare. Bob Russell and Dave Stone's dedication to this objective has been invaluable.

3. **You need to keep up with the numbers.** While the body of Christ is not about numbers for number's sake, it is important that you keep track of how many people are attending your programs, what is the median age of your congregation, what are the attendance trends, and other relevant factors. If you neglect this aspect of programming, you'll not be able to determine how well you're doing or the relative impact of new classes and programs.

4. **Successful churches follow up visitors and new members with phone calls and letters.** Again, we do this well, I think. In

his book, *Exit Interviews*, William Hendricks cites a study by Dr. John Savage which found that, not too surprisingly, people drop out of church because after they join they are ignored, overlooked, and not made to feel a part of the church body.[7]

 5. **There must be a logical, thoughtful process of involvement where each next step is identified and apparent to the new member.** You should always be seeking to learn the next step in your process. As you add new programs, it is essential that you understand where it fits into the overall scheme of things. More importantly, every new member needs to understand his or her next step.

 These general principles became the foundation for our assimilation process and the model we developed to illustrate the process.

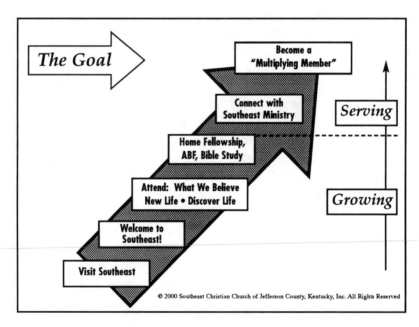

Chart 5: The Original Southeast Assimilation Model

PROGRAM MODELS

When I was given the job of Involvement Minister, I searched extensively for a model or program we could use. There are many. Willow Creek developed the Network program that is available through the Willow Creek Association. Bruce Bugbee, originally with Willow Creek, has his own Network Ministries model with supporting materials. Also, Leadership Network, an organization founded by Bob Buford in the early '90s in conjunction with Willow Creek, offers "A New Member's Starter Kit," which a lot of churches use. This is a wonderful resource with an enormous amount of assimilation information. The assimilation model used by Saddleback Community Church and outlined in Rick Warren's book, *The Purpose Driven Church*, is perhaps the most widely used.

Actually, the process of selecting an assimilation program was greatly facilitated by my boss at the time, Greg Tatum, who had recently joined the Southeast staff from East 91st Street Christian Church in Indianapolis. He brought with him a fully mature program that we could adapt to our needs. (To be honest, I really liked the Saddleback model, affectionately called the "Holy Baseball Diamond" by some. It is elegant in its simplicity, logical, and captivating.) Since Greg was my boss, I thought, "I'll humor him!" When I first met Greg, he tried to put me at ease by telling me: "Don't think of me as a boss. Just think of me as a friend who's always right."

Anyway, we used much of the basic framework and many ideas of East 91st Street, and I'm happy we did because, as we adapted the East 91st Street program to our specific circumstances, the model became uniquely ours reflecting Southeast's vision, values, and character. I encourage you to start with an existing program, maybe ours or maybe one of the other excellent ones. Regardless of the specific one you select, **I believe you will be wise to adapt, modify, and tailor the basic program to make it uniquely yours.** I am convinced it will make your assimilation process much more effective.

I still remember those early days when our program was in the embryonic stages. We had thirty days to field a program in its entirety, and the pressure was great. I would have killed (just a figure of speech) to have had something on a disk I could start with, but I couldn't find anything at the time. For that reason I typed every word personally. Hoping to save some poor soul reading this book the same ordeal, we have provided an Internet download with this book that contains every word of our current program. (See page 160 for access information.) You can print it out from your computer, replace "Southeast" with the name of your church or, better yet, take a few additional moments and adapt the program to the specific needs of your church.

The Arrow Model

Initially, we elected to portray our process as an upward arrow (see Chart 5). Some churches have developed a top-down model, but we thought one pointing heavenward would be more appropriate. The logic underlying the "Arrow Model" was that Southeast was a place for new members to *grow* in their relationship with Christ and *serve* Him by using their spiritual gifts to build up the body of Christ in this church. We bill Southeast as "A Place to Grow and a Place to Serve." The model began with a person visiting Southeast and perhaps attending our guest reception which I'll discuss later. The first step in growth was to attend our *Welcome to Southeast! (WTS!)* program that provides an overview of our church, its programs and ministries. As the new member seeks to grow, we offer several classes to that end which also will be discussed later.

Continuing in the process, new members would join an Adult Bible Fellowship (ABF, our adult Bible School program) or small group, connect to a ministry, and finally, and ideally, reach such a level of maturity that they would become a "multiplying member" and begin bringing others to Christ and to the Church. The model was helpful in that it graphically portrayed how we planned to administer our involvement program. However, while it accommodated entry at any point in the process depending on the maturity of the new member, it left people hanging, at least visually, when they reached the top. Another criticism I had of this model and most of the others I studied was that they only depicted the new member process after the person became a member. They didn't address the entirety of the process from the first time a guest entered the church campus until he or she became a member and was subsequently involved in the work of the church.

I know I keep using the word "process." I do this because I believe it is key to the success of any organizational endeavor. Both religious and secular institutions are inclined to pursue programs, to focus on a single component of an activity. Certainly this is easier to do from a management point of view, and the church is particularly vulnerable to this pitfall because of the discontinuity created by reliance on nonstaff members to get the job done.

Nevertheless, **unless programs are integrated within the framework of a larger context and founded on the organization's mission, vision, and values, they often disappear into obscurity after the next new program comes along.** I cynically refer to these as "Programs of the Month," and it is a common preoccupation of most churches and results in inefficient use of resources and the inevitable frustration and burnout. The scenario is a common one. Some energetic and well-intended staff member reads a book or attends a conference and is inspired to implement a new program that they are confident will be the 21st-century equivalent of the Protestant Reformation.

Unfortunately after some initial success and much fanfare, their initiative is soon supplanted by the program of another staff member who just returned from a conference with the next "Program of the Month." Successful organizations institutionalize their programs within the context of processes that are subscribed to by the senior leadership and are interrelated with organizational values and guiding principles.

The Wheel Model

After ten months of using the "arrow" model and assessing other approaches, we developed what I'll call "the wheel model." It really is an amalgamation of input from many different sources, and it wasn't crystallized until we were given the task to present a day-and-a-half new member seminar in conjunction with our biannual leadership conference. Previously, the evangelism portion of the New Members ministry and the involvement portion were loosely related but never fully integrated. When we were required to speak together and tell the entire new member story, the pieces began to fall in place and the model depicted below was developed.

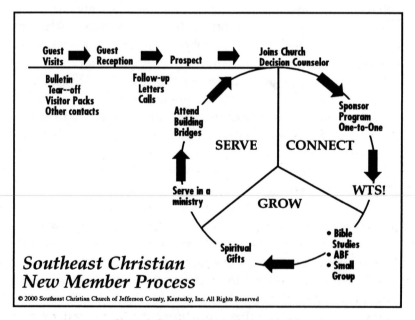

Chart 6: Southeast Assimilation Model

Guest Visits/Guest Reception

While I think the model is self-explanatory for the most part, I'd like to walk you through it since it will form the framework for the rest of this book. Though Guest Services is not a part of the New Member ministry, our efforts are inextricably linked. **When you're as large as Southeast, it is imperative that you overcompensate in the friendliness area.** We'll discuss the process of getting them in the front door and being super friendly in Chapter 5. We hope to get all of our guests to go through the guest reception conducted in our Fireside Room after every service. During the reception, guests get to meet one of our two most senior ministers, socialize, and have their questions answered by members of the congregation and staff. The guest reception will be addressed in Chapter 6.

Prospect/Membership

Once we become aware of a guest, either by their signing the guest register, completing a bulletin contact sheet, or other means, they become a prospect and an elaborate process of follow-up begins. That process is described in Chapter 7. The objective of all of these efforts is to have a guest either accept Jesus Christ as their Lord and Savior or, if they are already a believer, have them join the church and become a member. The decision counselor process, described in Chapter 8, has proven to be a highly effective tool to this end.

Involvement Stages

Essentially, the evangelism process gets the person to membership or to the baptistery. At that time, the involvement process begins. It consists of three stages: connect (Chapter 10), grow (Chapter 11), and serve (Chapter 12). These are depicted as a wheel, which I think is a useful metaphor since it suggests that once a person becomes a member, they enter a never-ending process viewed in two respects. **As individual Christians we are forever connecting to new areas of the church, growing/maturing in our relationship with God, and serving Him in some endeavor as part of the body of Christ.** The process is also never ending in that new members connect, grow, and serve and become sufficiently mature to be able to lead others to Christ or membership, and those new members then connect, grow, and serve. We offer this model for you to incorporate into your church activities or to adapt to your particular circumstances of your church.

ALTERNATE ROUTES

Any time you put a precisely delineated model on a piece of paper, you run the risk of oversimplifying. It never works as clearly as it appears on paper, and that's to be expected. What we're seeking is a process, a plan that points us in the right direction. In fact, the new member process we have developed accommodates multiple points of entry into involvement. We have had some new members who followed the process exactly from their first visit to guest reception to joining the church through *WTS!*, Spiritual Gifts, and involvement in the Guest Service Ministry.

Others follow a different route. I recall one couple in particular. Both were in their sixties and recently remarried. I first met Pat and Wilbur when they showed up at my Adult Bible Fellowship (ABF) class at 8:00 a.m. on Sunday. I next saw them at the *WTS!* program I was teaching at 9:15. Immediately afterwards I rushed to the Guest Reception where I was introducing guests to Bob Russell. I noticed that Pat and Wilbur were standing in line to meet Bob. When they made their way to the front of the line, I joked that they were doing the "new member thing" backwards. The model is supposed to lead you step by step to greater involvement. Since they were doing the model backwards, I was afraid that their next step was out the front door to the church down the street.

Another way of getting involved is quite common among mature Christians who transfer their membership from another church where they were active. They take it upon themselves to find their own place. I see them in the guest reception, we talk, and before you know it, they're singing in the choir, working in the parking lot, and giving the associate minister theological advice on sermon preparation. (Just kidding!)

LOOKING AHEAD

Obviously the model doesn't work as neatly as it appears on the page. It leaks. People disappear into the anonymity of the masses and don't get involved, or they slip out the back door to go to a church that better meets their needs. In Chapter 13 we'll talk about "closing the back door" or reducing the number of people who leave your church for reasons you could probably have prevented.

The model we adopted has been tailored to our particular circumstances, and we appreciate that not all churches face the same challenges and opportunities. For that reason, in Chapter 14 we will suggest how you might apply the model at your church depending on your unique situation — big church, small church, or in between, just getting started with a new member program, church attendance growing, plateaued, or declining. I think the model can work for you if you adapt it to your particular circumstances.

In Chapter 15 we will tell you how we did. As with any human endeavor, it's been a mixed bag. There have been some notable successes and some abject failures. **We have been ruthless in discarding what didn't work and trying something new,** and I hope we can spare you some misfortune by sharing our problems candidly.

Chapter 16 will peer into the future and share our thinking on how church assimilation programs need to be adapted to reach out to a generation of new believers living in a new millennium. We will briefly review the characteristics of the Generation X group, discuss postmodernism, and share with you our plans for more effectively sharing the gospel in this new environment and involving a new generation of new members.

In addition to the "words of wisdom" that we'll share in the chapters that follow, I have attempted to include an example of every document we developed during the formation of our assimilation program. These are included on the College Press website at *www.collegepress.com* and are downloadable. Let me offer a word of caution with regard to the documents contained here. You will want to read these letters and forms carefully before you use them. They are not necessarily formatted exactly as we use them in hard copies; they have been formatted for appearance on the computer. For that reason you may have to reformat, change margins, tabs, line spacing, etc. Finally, I have removed almost all of the artwork, logos, and pictures. You should embellish your final presentation with some attractive and appropriate art.

While we have copyrighted this information, you have permission to reprint, insert the name of your church where appropriate, and to use the material in any manner you wish as long as you agree that the material first belonged to Southeast Christian Church and do not charge for its use.

Part Two

MAKING YOUR CHURCH A PLACE TO GROW

Chapter 5

We Make New Members the Old Fashioned Way – We Invite Them

Philip found Nathanael and told him, "We have found the one Moses wrote about in the Law, and about whom the prophets also wrote—Jesus of Nazareth, the son of Joseph."

"Nazareth! Can anything good come from there?" Nathanael asked.

"Come and see," said Philip. John 1:45,46

Church growth is simple when you really think about it. All you have to do is get people to visit your church once and then make the experience so wonderful they'll want to come back and get involved. Like so many simple formulas however, in reality the problem is very difficult. Baron von Clausewitz, the world's preeminent theorist on the Art of War, made a similar observation about warfare. Clausewitz said, "In war everything is simple, but the simplest thing is very difficult." As far as I know, Clausewitz was able to discover this truism without ever attending a church board meeting, but his insights have great application to much of what we do in church.

Nevertheless the very first step in the assimilation process is getting new people to come to church in the first place. Since this is such a crucial factor, I have made a point of asking every guest or visitor I meet what first attracted them to Southeast. Over time I have compiled a list of these reasons and I'll share that list with you à la David Letterman style. The first four or five may be in jest, but reasons five through one are for real and, I think, valid.

THE TOP TEN REASONS
PEOPLE COME TO SOUTHEAST

Reason number 10. They were looking for Rupp Arena, the University of Kentucky basketball stadium. These people usually arrived in a 1970s vintage pickup truck with a "Go Big Blue" bumper sticker on the back. True enough there are some similarities in the appearance of the two facilities, and since Kentucky is such a basketball crazed state, I could almost believe it.

Reason number 9. They were part of the construction crew working on the building. It seemed to us that some of these guys were never going to complete their part of the new building. We joked that since they were going to spend the rest of their professional lives at Southeast, it was easier for them to just become members. In truth, we did have a number of the workers join the church and become active members.

Reason number 8. Some visitors were attracted by the theater seats at Southeast that were more comfortable than the pews at their former church. Again there is an element of truth here. Our sanctuary is arranged in a semicircle and because of its size (it seats just under 9000) would have required curved pews that were prohibitively expensive. Thus we elected to go with theater seats that present a less "churchy" appearance. Seekers feel more comfortable in an environment that doesn't look "high church." Perhaps just for tradition's sake we did preserve about 10 percent of our seating as pews, mostly near the back of the sanctuary.

Reason number 7. They wanted to see what Bob looked like. We often tease our senior minister because his stature is closer to David's than Goliath's. One lady joked that she had heard him on the radio and wanted to see him in person. She said he wasn't as tall as he sounded on the radio.

Reason number 6. True story. We have a huge number of people assisting people in the parking lot and a couple of guys who help coordinate traffic for people wishing to drop passengers off at the front entrance. Soon after we moved in, one of our volunteer traffic coordinators encountered a driver who had stopped under the portico and was creating a traffic jam. The traffic coordinator approached the driver and asked him politely to move on. The driver was angry and rolled down his window and said that he did not want to come to church, he just wanted directions to Cracker Barrel, a nearby restaurant. In fact, he had gotten off the Interstate intending to go to Cracker Barrel but had gotten caught up (should we say "raptured"?) in the traffic coming to Southeast on a Sunday morning and now **he was lost**. We told him we were in the business of saving the lost and offered him some spiritual food, but he declined seeking the higher cholesterol variety of food.

Reason number 5. A common reason given for first attending Southeast is that **the visitors were just curious.** They had seen the building under construction and thought they'd come and check it out to see what was happening at 920 Blankenbaker Parkway. How can your church arouse the curiosity of people in your community? A building program is one way. Special programs are also effective. More than anything else people sense when something exciting is happening and want to find out more. Creating a sense of excitement and helping your congregation catch the excitement is key.

Reason number 4. Their kids "brought" them. I was fascinated by how often this was mentioned as a reason for first attending Southeast. In most cases, teenagers began attending youth programs after being invited by friends. They got so excited about their programs that the parents decided to come and see what was so special about the church. When they came, they stayed. In other cases, parents were just looking for a good youth program and were delighted when they found out how robust ours was.

Soon after we moved into our new building, I met a young, single mother who had become quite active in the church. "Ali," I asked, "why did you first come to Southeast?" "My daughter brought me," she said. Since her daughter was only three, I was a little perplexed until Ali explained. Before going to work in the morning, Ali would drop her daughter off at a nearby day care center and passed the church while it was under construction. Her daughter asked about the building and said she wanted to see it. After we had moved into our new building, Ali did visit. The day following her visit Ali's dad died, and she had no one to turn to for comfort. She came to the church and was greeted by a Welcome Center volunteer who was solicitous and understanding. This volunteer took Ali to see our minister on call where she received the comfort she so desperately needed at the time.

Another story related to the children's program points up the importance of attention to detail. One couple was looking for a church home and was actually looking for a church smaller than Southeast. But after shopping around, they visited Southeast. Their son was deathly allergic to peanuts, and we were the only church who asked about food allergies. The parents were impressed enough to join. The point to be made in all these examples is that there are many ways to attract people to your church. Survey your church's strengths. It could be a children's or youth program that leads a person to join your church.

Reason number 3. An embarrassingly large number of new members I talk to say that they came to Southeast because **they weren't being fed at their previous church.** Often the Bible isn't being taught. Frequently, the preaching or programming is shallow or not done with excellence. While I'm convinced that the Word of God is powerful and effective, it is important for us to communicate it in the most effective manner humanly possible. When that is not done, people are less likely to respond to it. Because a significant percentage of new members transfer their membership from another church, we are often accused of stealing members from other churches. That is simply not true. As Bob says: "We sow grass, we don't steal sheep."

There has been some controversy concerning megachurch growth. Christian researchers such as George Barna contend that the percentage of "born again" Christians has remained constant, suggesting that much of what is counted as "growth" is really only Christians moving their membership from one church to another. There is some truth to this assertion. We don't have any solid data on how Southeast is doing in this area. We do know that in 1999, we added 2,457 new members, 1300 by baptism and 1157 by transfer. In talking to a large number of these new members I believe that about half of the people who joined Southeast were virtually "unchurched." That is, that while they may fall into the category of "transfers," in fact their attendance at their former church was so infrequent that they were unchurched for all practical purposes. I don't know how church growth experts would classify these new members, but I'm inclined to think that "once they were lost, and now they are found." The same is true of those baptized. Not all were making a first time confession of faith in Jesus Christ, but many, perhaps most, had fallen away from the church to the point that they would have to be counted officially as unchurched.

Reason number 2. The guest had heard Bob on the radio and they liked what they heard. Bob's sermons are currently broadcast on over 44 radio stations, his sermons can be found on about a half dozen websites, and he is featured on two local radio stations. Obviously, his messages are well prepared, delivered with excellence, and speak to people in a convicting way. Of course, this is not accidental. Over the years, Bob has continued to devote 25-30 hours a week to sermon preparation and it makes a difference.

Reason number 1. (Drum roll please.) The number one reason people first attended Southeast was that **a friend invited them.** Often it's no more complicated than that. I think of Philip's experience with Nathanael in the first chapter of John. Philip was excited at meeting Jesus and ran to Nathanael saying that the one the prophets had promised had arrived. Nathanael was skeptical and asked, "Can anything good come out of Nazareth?" Philip's response was simple and effective. "Come and see," he said.

We conducted a congregational survey about eight months after moving into our new building, and the results confirmed this point. Over 94 percent of our members invited someone to Southeast during the past year. Like Philip, many of the members of our congregation are saying: "Come and see."

I think one of the most amazing facts about Southeast's growth over the years is that we have done very little to market the church or increase our profile in the community. While we have been committed to seeking and saving the lost in the Louisville area, we have not taken an inordinately active role in social issues. We have preached the truth in love and taken an unequivocal stand on some sensitive issues such as abortion, gambling, and homosexuality, but we haven't taken this fight to the press or attempted to intentionally increase our profile. Nor have we spent much of our resources on advertising, primarily due to space limitations. Until moving into our new building, we were so strapped for space that advertising would simply add to the overcrowding. We had as many people streaming in the door as we could handle, so we did not elect to spend our limited resources on TV, radio, or newspaper advertising.

The church sponsored several events annually that attracted large numbers of visitors. Clearly, the most prominent of these initiatives is the Easter pageant. What began as a relatively simple enactment of the gospel story that we performed during the Easter season became a hugely successful production over the years. Our most recent production attracted over 70,000 who came to see a professional performance by an all-volunteer cast featuring wonderful music, world class scenery, and a realistic depiction of Christ's life replete with camels, scores of Roman soldiers, and Jesus literally ascending five stories into the heavens at the program's climax. While many, perhaps most, came to be entertained, the program is overtly evangelistic and effective. In addition to the Easter Pageant, the Christmas program attracts thousands and we sponsor special speakers and programs throughout the year that assist us in getting new people in the doors of our church.

Once these people have stepped inside the doors of the church, we need to make sure that they feel welcome and that their needs are being met. This is no small challenge because of our size. But I would suggest that this is a high priority with any church regardless of its size. We all need a system that makes visitors (I mean guests) feel welcome. As we first attempted to develop an effective guest services ministry, the first thing we had to do was change our phraseology, and people like me had to purge the "V" word, "visitor," from our vocabulary.

Though widely used, "visitor" did not describe the way we wanted to regard the people who came to Southeast for the first time. "Visitor" suggests someone staying for a specified period of time before they move on. It's kind of like the board game Monopoly when you land on the corner jail square. In this case, you just want to be visiting before you move on to acquire Park Place or Boardwalk. When you invite someone into your house, you don't call them "visitors." You call them "guests" — unless they're in-laws in which case you might call them something else that rhymes with guests. "What's in a name?" Shakespeare asked — perhaps a lot when it comes to guests.

We have always acknowledged the importance of greeters at Southeast and were able to field scores of people to stand at the front door often in freezing temperature or sweltering heat to provide a first touch to arriving members and guests. But in 1998, we hired a Guest Services director and took guest services to a new level. While we have a paid staff of eight (counting receptionists) who administer our guest services ministry, it is probably the most volunteer-intensive operation we have. In addition to greeters, ushers, and people to hand out bulletins, Guest Services takes care of communion servers, has someone to give tours of the building throughout the week, and runs our two Leadership Conferences each year.

When we inaugurated our Guest Services program, it was clear that **people start forming an impression of our church well before they even enter the door.** With this reality in mind, we began encouraging our parking lot coordinators to be friendly and helpful while they were parking cars. Due to overcrowding and limited space, traffic has always been a problem for us, and some of our veteran parking lot workers maintain that it was hard to smile when people were trying to perform vehicular homicide on you on their way to worship God. Still, we were able to solicit their cooperation in being a positive first touch to arriving guests and new members. Of course we employed the standard first-time-visitor parking with the standard mixed results. Enforcing first-time-visitor parking is all but impossible without offending someone, and it's rumored that one of our charter members occasionally avails herself of a first-time-visitor slot. I hope I'm kidding, but you take my point, I'm sure.

We'd like for people to get five touches before they get to the sanctuary. Bob and Dave and other ministers often stand in the atrium and greet arriving worshipers. To provide another touch, we inaugurated a very successful program in 1998 called "Section Hosts." We noticed that, by and large, people tended to sit in the same general area of the sanctuary every time they attend. We identified a group of willing and outgoing volunteers who were assigned a particular section of the sanctuary, and it was their job to minister to that group. The section host merely arrived a little earlier and chatted with people before the service started. These volunteers are extremely effective in providing another touch.

In the next chapter, I'll detail how we get feedback from guests. In this chapter, I will share with you that the guest feedback we get about the warmth and friendliness of the church is hugely positive. I think a lot of this is due to the fact that the guest expects the enormous megachurch to be impersonal, and they are blown away by how warm, friendly, and engaging a big church can be. While this may appear effortless from the guest's point of view, it is an enormous undertaking but one you can implement at your church on a smaller scale.

Chapter 6

The Guest Reception: Where the Guest and the Preacher Come Together

Greet one another with a holy kiss. All the saints send their greetings. May the grace of the Lord Jesus Christ, and the love of God, and the fellowship of the Holy Spirit be with you all.

2 Corinthians 13:12-14

It's a familiar sight at many churches. We've all seen it. The Sunday morning worship service has just been completed, and the senior minister dutifully makes his way to the rear of the church to greet departing worshipers. An elderly lady who left the sanctuary before the invitation is waiting to speak with the minister and give him an earful about hymn selection or to ask him to pray for her festering case of bunions. The minister, not wanting to be rude to this regular tither, listens patiently while any number of guests or new members slip out the door without even a "how d'ya do" or "pleased to meet you."

Now clearly our established members need pastoring, but it is vitally important that guests and new members have an opportunity to make contact with the senior minister. A survey of 26 mainline U.S. congregations, which was published in the March 1996 issue of *Reformed Worship*, found that there were three primary reasons people gave for becoming a member of a particular church. Reason one was that the congregation acts like it really believes Jesus is alive. Reason two is that the pastor seems to believe what he preaches. Reason three was that the pastor seems personable by smiling, using humor appropriately, greeting people at the door, and other methods that allow personal contact with the guest.[8]

Writing for the Alban Institute, Roy M. Oswald and Speed B. Leas concluded that a distant pastor can have the opposite effect. In their book, *The Inviting Church: A Study of New Member Assimilation*, they said:

> As further evidence of the importance of the pastor in helping with the assimilation process, when we asked newcomers, "What almost kept you from joining the congregation?" the most frequent responses were: 1. I was ignored by the minister. 2. The sermons were poor. 3. The service was difficult to follow. In large churches it is probably impossible for the senior minister to greet and pay attention to all newcomers; however many newcomers still feel the need for attention from the pastor.[9]

To address this issue, Southeast inaugurated a Guest Reception when we moved into our new building in 1998. In retrospect it was probably the most successful innovation we initiated at the time. The purpose of the guest reception is threefold. First, and most important, it allows guests and new members an opportunity to come in personal contact with the senior minister. While this is really important for a large church, it is also critical for smaller churches.

Second, guests get another "touch" and have an opportunity to form relationships. This is absolutely essential in any church regardless of size. Win Arn maintains that, "Each new convert or new member should be able to identify at least seven friends in the church within the first six months. Friendships appear to be the strongest bond cementing new converts or members to their congregation."[10]

I've seen people exchanging phone numbers, making appointments to get together, and discovering long lost friends at our guest reception. We also have people coming to the guest reception who need to talk to a minister about a spiritual, family, or personal problem. For that reason we have a minister or lay counselor available at each guest reception. Often people elect to make a decision for Christ at the reception. I recall one Sunday in 1999 when we had nine people who gave their life to Christ or joined the church at the guest reception. Since there is a considerable walk between the Fireside Room, where we conduct the reception, and the decision counseling area, we now have several decision counselors on duty at the guest reception.

Third, new members can have their questions answered and get additional information about church programs. Here, knowledgeable volunteers form the nucleus of our effort. Most of the information about our various ministries and programs is available in brochures that are maintained in attractive displays. Still, there are so many options available, we have to have someone to assist guests and new members in finding the programs which are particularly suited to them.

Here's how the process works (refer to Chart 7 on the next page): While the worship team seeks to limit the number of pulpit announcements, after each service they invite guests and new members to drop by the Fireside Room to meet Bob and Dave. The benefit is threefold: It reminds everyone that guests are special; it discourages members and regular attenders from dropping in and monopolizing the pastors' time (occasionally some members drop in, but the process discourages a significant number of nonguests); the pulpit announcement educates the rest of the congregation that the guest reception is a value to the church. As a consequence, our members are more inclined to encourage guests to drop by the Fireside Room.

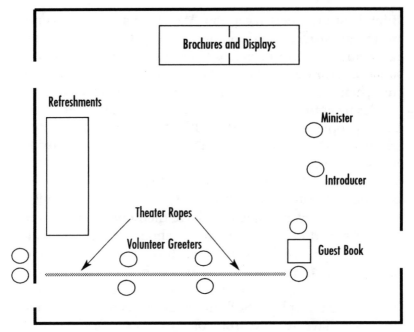

Chart 7: Guest Reception Set-up

THE GUEST ROOM

The room is prominently identified as "Guest Reception." A volunteer is stationed just outside the door to invite passersby in and provides one more touch to those who enter. We use theater ropes for crowd control, and they are placed so as to form a line which leads to a guest register. No one seems to object to the line even though it may mean a fifteen minute wait when an exceptional number of guests show up. We station volunteers on the other side of the rope to chat with guests while they wait. We are currently trying a new arrangement with the brochures and display tables taking the place of the theater ropes. The advantage of this set-up is that guests have an opportunity to browse for information while they wait.

A critical stop in the process is the guest book. We have a volunteer who stands at the guest book to greet the individuals, encourage them to sign in, and give them an attractive invitation to attend *Welcome to Southeast!* (See invitation at Appendix 1.) **When guests sign the guest book, they cease to be guests and become prospects.** We ask for name, address, and phone number, and this information is later compiled on a spreadsheet. Each guest from the local area subsequently receives a letter with relevant information enclosed. Out-of-towners receive only a letter thanking them for attending Southeast. (These letters will be discussed in the next chapter.) Generally, about ⅔ of guest reception attenders are from the local area.

Once the person has signed the guest book, they move to the next station where a minister talks with them briefly until either Bob or Dave is ready to speak with them. The first minister acts as a screener of sorts in that he discourages members from interfering with the process. This requires a good deal of discernment since we want to honor our membership without allowing Bob or Dave to get bogged down with nonguest related activities. The screener is also alert for individuals who may want to burden Bob or Dave with a lengthy personal problem or spiritual concern. Frequently, these people are diverted to another minister who listens to the problem, prays with the individual and perhaps sets up an appointment for follow-up counseling. Both Bob and Dave devote quality time with each person and the meeting usually takes between one and three minutes.

After the guest has met with Bob or Dave they can partake of refreshments, mingle with church volunteers or peruse church information available in attractive displays. We also provide gifts of Southeast coffee cups and refrigerator magnets with essential church information on it.

The guest reception is my favorite place to be on a weekend. I get energized by the people attending the guest reception, and I am impressed by their enthusiasm. I recall one person in particular. Her name is Cheryl. She was standing in line to sign the guest book when I approached her and asked if she were a guest. "Oh, no," Cheryl responded emphatically, "I have been attending for a month, but these are my guests," and she introduced me to a young couple she invited to attend service with her. The next week I saw Cheryl again at the guest reception. This time she had brought another friend to church. I was more than a little chagrined that this new member had invited more people to Southeast in two weeks than I had invited in two years.

As an outgrowth of the Guest Reception, we recently added a procedure to keep up with guests who visit the church during the week. We have a large number of visitors, tour groups, and curiosity seekers during the week. For that reason the Welcome Center is manned with volunteers during normal operating hours and tour guides are standing by. A certain percentage of our "drop-in" visitors are considering making Southeast their home or at least might worship with us if encouraged to do so. For this reason, Welcome Center volunteers and tour guides encourage visitors to worship with us. In addition, when appropriate, we ask that visitors sign in on a guest book maintained at the reception center. We then follow up their visit with a phone call seeking to answer any questions and to encourage the individual to join us for worship on the weekend.

Regardless of the size of your church, a guest reception can be a helpful addition. The organization inherent in the process makes the best possible use of the pastor's time while allowing guests, new members, and existing members an opportunity to chat with the minister and learn more about the church if desired.

Chapter 7

The Three Ps of Prospecting: People, Persistence, and Paperwork

---

Go rather to the lost sheep of Israel. As you go, preach this message: '"The kingdom of heaven is near." Matthew 10:6,7

The discussion thus far has centered on getting new people into the church and making them feel welcome. Aside from making them feel welcome, however, we also want to do everything within our power to lead them to a saving relationship with Jesus Christ and/or church membership. In some cases this happens automatically, with little involvement on behalf of anyone but the Holy Spirit. For whatever reason, a person comes forward after a service and talks to a decision counselor who explains the plan of salvation and completes the paperwork for church membership. This process is described in Chapter 8.

But for a large number of people, the process of becoming a member is long and involved. As a matter of fact, we had one lady who took 14 years before she was ready to commit to church membership. In January 2000 we began asking new members when they first began attending Southeast. The median amount of time between first visit and joining the church was 18 months. I've asked a number of people why so much time elapsed and discovered that there was nothing specific.

My personal feeling is that we are slower to commit to anything today than we were, say 25 years ago. Our personal lives are hectic and our schedules are packed. Church is one more activity that competes for our time, and it is no longer considered an essential part of our lives for many. If, however, people will continue to attend, at some point, at a time of God's own choosing, they may take the step of faith. It may be after attending once; it may be after attending for 14 years. The point is that it is God's timing, not ours. Obviously, we try to do everything in our power to assist people in making that commitment, but it simply takes time. As we will see in Chapter 16, it is likely that future Americans will be even slower to make a commitment to church membership.

The process of converting guests into new members begins when we get someone's name. Whether you are talking about a megachurch or a smaller church, getting a name is not as easy as it sounds because many are protective about their anonymity and don't want to become part of someone's mailing list. And, we don't want to just make them part of a list either. Rather we want to share with them the eternal, life-saving gospel message of truth and salvation. Though many are not quick to surrender their name, we are determined to follow-up with guests if at all possible.

GETTING NAMES

Unlike many churches, Southeast does not take attendance, though it would make the new member minister's job easier if we did. How then do we get a person's name?

1. As described in the last chapter, **the guest reception is a rich source of prospects.** That's why we encourage everyone to sign in on the guest book, and most of the people who take the initiative to go to the guest reception, don't mind providing their name and phone number.

2. **The bulletin tear-off sheet.** Every bulletin has a page for guests that can be detached (Appendix 2). The front side

provides useful information for guests. We tell them not to feel obligated to participate in the offering, and we also describe the communion process to avoid those awkward moments when communion is passed. Since practices vary from church to church, we are committed to clarify our procedures so our guests will be more comfortable.

The tear-off sheet also gives some helpful hints for people with children. Again, children's involvement in the worship service varies significantly from church to church, and we want to help the guest (and our members too) understand what the expectation is for children who attend the worship service. We believe everyone will be more comfortable if children stay in the nursery or participate in a children's program. We advise parents of the availability of cry-rooms, too.

On the flip side of the tear-off sheet is a form that allows our guests to request a wide variety of information from how they can come to a relationship with Jesus Christ as Lord and Savior to subscribing to our weekly newspaper, *The Outlook*, or volunteering in a ministry. We get half of our most promising prospects from the tear-off sheets. It is a minor but important point that each weekend's tear-off sheet is dated so the office staff will know when the guest attended church at Southeast.

3. The third source of information comes from **a feedback card contained in a booklet we distribute to first-time guests.** For many years now we have published an attractive and professional-looking four-color booklet that provides an overview of Southeast, our beliefs, people, and ministries. Copies are distributed at the end of each service to first-time visitors. The worship leader merely asks anyone wanting to learn more about the church to raise their hand as the ushers make their way up the aisle.

This process isn't overly threatening to a guest who may want to preserve a modicum of anonymity, but at the same time, their identity is revealed to the people sitting around them who should greet them and make them feel welcome. Included in these packets is a copy of *The Outlook* and an audio tape with a greeting from our minister and worship music on one side, and a sermon on "How to Become a Christian" on the other side. We distribute between 250 and 300 of these first-time visitor packets each weekend.

One page of the "Welcome to Southeast!" booklet is a postage- and fees-paid postcard requesting feedback from the guest. If the guest will take the time to complete and return the postcard, we send them a copy of "The Bible Promise Book." We are exceedingly eager to get their feedback, but even more eager to get their names so we can start helping them decide to become part of the awesome work God is doing here in the Louisville area.

These cards really do work in getting new names and providing some feedback. Overall, the feedback is disproportionately positive, and we don't get as much constructive criticism as we'd like. Nevertheless, every time we do get a useful piece of constructive criticism, we attempt to resolve the issue aggressively. During our most recent revision of the booklet, we reduced the size and location of the postcard making it less apparent to the guest. The number of returned cards was reduced significantly, and we plan to make the card more prominent with the next revision and make sure that it does not have to be detached so people will be more inclined to complete the information and return the card.

Once we have a name, an elaborate, methodical process of follow-up begins that is depicted by the diagram below and will be described in the pages that follow. Since this process is very labor and paperwork intensive, it's easy to neglect it and focus your energy on more glamorous endeavors. But in the area of helping people make a decision for Christ, join the church or get involved once they are members, the letters, mailings, phone calls, and voicemail messages are a critical component of the process. Our schedule is depicted below:

Weekend	Monday	Tuesday	Thursday
Bulletin tear-off forms completed	Material collected, letters prepared	Letter to callers prepared	Callers receive list of people
Decision Counseling sheets filled out	Letter for guest reception attendees	Letter to guests and new members sent	to be called
Guest reception book filled in	Prospects and new member data into computer		

Chart 8: Schedule of Guest Follow-up

It's not enough to simply mail out a bunch of material. The process has to be logical and consistent, and it must make multiple, timely contacts with guests and new members. Our goal is to make written and verbal contact with every prospect within five days. Many church growth experts suggest contact needs to be made within 36 hours but we have been unable to achieve that goal to date.

Of course our ministers are constantly interacting with individuals seeking to make a decision for Christ or seeking information about church membership. Our New Member staff of Esther, Kindra, and Susie also spend countless hours on the phone helping people make a decision to commit their lives to Jesus or to the church. I cannot overstate the passion and effectiveness of these Christian soldiers in doing the Lord's work.

On Monday morning, the New Member staff begins to assemble all the materials from the weekend. Each person who completes a bulletin tear-off, attends the Guest Reception, returns a questionnaire from our visitor packet, or calls wanting information about attending Southeast, is profiled in our computer system under "Prospects" with a specific mailing profile code. Prospects are called or sent information about upcoming events and sermon series. Generally we maintain this data for two years, figuring that if a person hasn't joined or become involved by then, additional calls and letters probably won't help. When profiling is complete, a large number of letters are prepared to be sent to guests and new members.

Samples of these letters are contained in Appendixes 3–11. Specifically we send the following letters by Thursday of each week:

Subject/Inquiry	Who signs
Letter for a person who calls for information about the church	New Member secretary
First-time guest	Senior Minister
Someone interested in our beliefs	New Member Minister
Interested in membership	New Member Minister
Interested in membership (unable to reach by phone)	New Member Minister
Interested in baptism	New Member Minister
Letter to out-of-town visitor	Senior Minister
Attended guest reception	Involvement Minister
Letter to person completing and returning questionnaire	New Member Minister

The above letters are amended to meet specific requests when necessary.

While letters are reasonably effective in communicating information to guests and new members, phone calls provide a more personal touch. For this reason, Southeast has developed an elaborate phone calling program that involves dozens of callers in several different endeavors.

The most formal volunteer calling program we have consists of about 50 volunteers who call people from their homes. We conduct training periodically through the year so callers know how to maximize the effectiveness of their calls. The calls are carefully scripted, and we try to be as helpful to our volunteers as possible. Again, there is a lot of paperwork associated with this process, and we are interested in responding as soon as possible.

The volunteer callers are sent a copy of the bulletin tear-off or decision counseling sheet so they are aware of the person's interests or needs. Information of a personal nature is deleted. Callers are also informed of what information we have sent the person so that they can help with any questions that might arise. In addition to the calls and letters, we also refer any specific request to the applicable ministry so individuals can be contacted as appropriate.

The biggest challenge is keeping the lay callers abreast of the new programs and opportunities in which new people can participate. Another challenge is keeping up with programs that change. Calls to those interested in membership (Appendix 14) are a good example of what we are trying to achieve with our calls. We ask callers to smile during the call. You wouldn't think that whether a caller smiles or not would make any difference, but **psychologists maintain that smiling subconsciously influences the attitude of the caller and hence the phone conversation.** We also ask the caller to pray first. Obviously, praying is of utmost importance so we can involve God in the conversation. Likewise a few hints on telephone curiosity are provided to remind the volunteer not to be too intrusive. As you can imagine, our callers get hit with all kinds of questions and responses. They are encouraged to answer what they feel comfortable dealing with and refer difficult questions to a minister. (See Appendixes 12–15 for calling-related attachments.)

It should be no surprise that the biggest challenge by far is the answering machine. We ask our callers to try twice to make contact with a real person, but if they can't on the third attempt to leave a voice message. The caller is instructed to ask the prospect for a return call, but they also are to leave the information necessary for the person to discern what the call was about. We get great feedback from this program. The callers call and report to the new member secretary, especially if additional information is needed. They send the completed sheets back to her, so there is accountability for the calls.

We have some awesome callers. Their stories of persistence and compassion are legendary. In a time when many crave human contact and others have deep, festering personal problems that require no more complicated therapy than someone willing to listen, our caller's assistance extends far beyond simply calling to say, "Welcome to Southeast!"

I'm sure it's possible to provide too much information, but we want to make contact with as many people as possible through as many channels as possible, such as mail, e-mail, phones, postcards, and the church newspaper. Because we felt like we still weren't getting through to everyone, we began publishing a monthly new member and guest newsletter called "The Spotlight" (Appendix 16). The purpose of this publication was to highlight information of particular interest to the guest and new member and has been successful in doing so.

Clearly, not every church is called to contend with 200 new members a month and 250-300 first-time guests each week. But as Christ points out in the parable of the talents, **we are expected to make the best use of the resources we've been given and the prospects God sends our way.** The process I have described helps regardless of the number of prospects you have or the size of your congregation.

I should add in closing this chapter that Southeast has no formal program to visit individuals in their homes. While some individuals may take the initiative to visit guests and new members in their homes from time to time, this effort hasn't been encouraged. The rationale for this policy is that Americans are increasingly reluctant to open their homes to strangers. I think our unwillingness to open our home to strangers began to increase as our communities diminished in importance. Gone are the days when you would drop in on neighbors or welcome the interruption of an unexpected caller from the church. For better or worse, we have become more insulated and isolated and for these reasons we have no home visitation program.

Chapter 8

Decision Counseling: The Linchpin of the New Member Process

This is good, and pleases God our Savior, who wants all men to be saved and to come to a knowledge of the truth.
1 Timothy 2:3,4

In my 28 years of service in the United States Air Force, my family and I moved 22 times. Each time we moved we would place our membership in the local church where we lived. Generally the process was simple, straightforward, and, regrettably, superficial. At the end of the service, the congregation would sing a hymn of invitation and my family and I would walk forward. While the congregation was singing, I would fill out the appropriate paperwork detailing the particulars of names, addresses, phone numbers, and past church affiliation. At the conclusion of the singing, the minister would welcome us to the congregation and encourage everyone to come forward and meet us. In some cases we were asked to repeat the Good Confession before the congregation. And that was it. We were members.

In 1995, my wife and I rejoined Southeast, quite unexpectedly. We had planned to retire in Florida after I left the service. We had a retirement home in Fort Walton Beach and were prepared to live out our days in the sunny south. God had other plans, and we were inexorably drawn back to

Louisville and our home church. We were visiting my parents in Louisville when God made His will so clear to us. I can remember the day Nancy and I felt the call. I can remember the exact pew we were sitting in during a worship service at Southeast when we felt the presence of the Holy Spirit tugging at us individually.

Still in the Air Force and living in Alabama, Nancy and I were chatting as we made our way back home. We were on I-65 just south of Nashville when I said, "How would you feel about retiring in Louisville instead of Florida." Nancy admitted she had been thinking the same thing. The next week we put our Florida home on the market and prepared to move back to my hometown. Subsequently, I was hired by the church to be Director of Facilities, and the rest is history. Occasionally, when it's 20 degrees and snowing, I have second thoughts, but I am so glad God led us back to Southeast.

Based on our previous experience joining other churches, we had an expectation of the process that was going to take place when we went forward to transfer our membership back to our home church. We were surprised. First, Bob Russell, who was a longtime friend of the family and who married Nancy and me in 1967, greeted us when we came forward by saying, "What are you doing here?" That seemed like a peculiar greeting for someone wanting to make a decision for Christ, but I admittedly caught him by surprise. Bob made pleasant conversation for a moment and then introduced Nancy and me to decision counselors who escorted us, separately, to a private area where we could chat. I must confess that even though I have been a Christian for my entire life, I was a little intimidated by the process that followed.

I had expected to fill out some paperwork and perhaps repeat the Good Confession. What transpired was a thorough and effective review of my walk with Christ and an introduction to some of the programs available at Southeast. To be honest, I felt a little ill at ease. The interview was personal, and we talked about deeply spiritual matters. The decision counselor reviewed the plan of salvation and asked me where I was in my relationship with Christ.

Since that time **I have come to appreciate how important the decision counseling process is in assimilating new members because it gets them off on the right spiritual foot.** It makes a statement at the beginning of a new member's involvement with the church that first and foremost being a member of Southeast Christian Church is about having a personal relationship with Jesus Christ. Participation in programs, volunteering, and working at the church are fine, but Christ is first. I cannot begin to overstate the importance of a comprehensive decision counseling program.

The purpose of the process is threefold: *One,* to lead a person to a saving relationship or closer walk with Jesus Christ; *two,* to make personal contact with the individual coming forward; and *three,* to help them determine their next step in the process of becoming a fully assimilated member of the local church. In pointing to the next step we discovered that it is not helpful to inundate the new member with a lot of information. That was our initial, though misguided, inclination.

To be honest, people are not too receptive at this time. First, for many (like me) it is a fairly intimidating experience. They are talking to a stranger about very personal and deeply spiritual matters, and that generally doesn't put a person at ease. Secondly, there's just too much information that the new member needs. It's impossible to do it justice in a 20-45 minute session. We found that the best approach was to hand them a card (Appendix 18) that outlined the available programs and said, "Your next step is _____" (fill in the blank).

ASSESSING THE CHRIST RELATIONSHIP

We haven't always had a comprehensive decision counseling program. For years, we had a process similar to the one I described earlier. However, in the mid-'80s the church leadership felt the need for a more formal, more intentional program. The process starts by recognizing that people respond to the invitation for a variety of reasons. A certain percentage come forward to make an initial commitment to Christ as Lord and Savior and to be baptized. Others come forward to rededicate themselves to Christ. Most often the intention is to join the church, to unite in fellowship, and these people come from a variety of backgrounds and from varied levels of spiritual maturity. Our requirements for membership are:

1) *Receive Jesus and His gift of salvation as a free gift.*
2) *Repent,* which means to change our minds about how to live this life. We must decide to live God's way.
3) *Confess,* which means to admit we have sinned and are willing to confess Jesus Christ as Lord and Savior.
4) *Be immersed.* We believe baptism by immersion should take place when a person has fulfilled all the above steps. In requiring baptism by immersion for membership, our intent is not to demean the individual's initial baptism, but rather to point out that the first-century prototype was most assuredly by immersion. This can be a hang-up for many, and our database contains about a hundred people a year waiting for the right time to get baptized.

Another concern is that Southeast has increasingly become "the thing to do" for many. We want to help people understand that while we are happy for them to join the church, our primary goal is to help them develop a personal relationship with Jesus Christ. That's why we ask a series of questions at the very beginning. Why did you come forward today? If you died today, what would happen to you? etc. After assessing the motivation of the person coming forward, the counselor then knows how deeply to get into the plan of salvation.

The procedures surrounding baptism are really a process in itself. **We encourage people to be baptized as soon as possible**, providing they are ready spiritually, of course. For that reason, we have all the necessary clothing available so the individual can go directly from the decision counseling area to the dressing room and into the baptistery without having to bring any personal articles with them from home. Once they are baptized, the new member receives a personalized Bible.

TRAINING THE COUNSELORS

All this requires a large group of spiritually mature and trained counselors, and we currently have about 200 trained counselors. The selection and training of decision counselors is a serious process that takes commitment and hard work, but the rewards are worth the investment of time and energy. The process begins with the selection of candidates to be counselors. The first requirement is that they be spiritually mature and a Southeast member for at least one year. For this reason we do not advertise for counselors nor do we recruit from the congregation. Rather the need is communicated by word of mouth, and people are usually nominated by ministers, ABF leaders, Home Bible Fellowship leaders and existing counselors.

Candidates need to know their spiritual gifts and temperament so participation in our *Discover Your Spiritual Gifts* class is encouraged. We wouldn't exclude anyone because of their temperament or gifts, but we know that certain combinations are most helpful in leading someone to Christ. Obviously, the gift of evangelism is nice, but discernment, faith, mercy, leadership, and wisdom are also helpful. Likewise, any temperament can do the job, but Melancholies and Phlegmatics are probably best suited to the task.

Each person seeking to become a decision counselor completes an application (Appendix 17) and is scheduled for an interview. These interviews are conducted by the New Member Minister and usually take about 30 minutes to an hour. The interviews consist of prayer, a general discussion of the applicant's spiritual background, their motives for wanting to be a decision counselor, and a general outline of the expectations for the job.

When approved, the applicant goes through an extensive training program. This training is conducted two to three times a year with a class size of about 10 to 15 to allow for an open learning environment. Most often the classes are held on Sunday afternoon from 3:00 to 7:00. Our New Member minister, Les Hughes, is the instructor, and he covers the material that deftly introduces the aspirant to how to gently but firmly lead a person to Christ. I think most mature Christians understand the plan of salvation, but using the Bridge Illustration in leading another person to reach a decision requires wisdom and discernment as well as knowledge. The training involves role playing and helpful answers for just about every possible question. Since baptism by immersion is frequently the most controversial issue, we spend extra time on that subject. We also discuss how to deal with other issues such as individuals living together outside of marriage.

Once the training is completed, new counselors watch a veteran go through a session or two and then they have someone look over their shoulder during their initial counseling sessions. In addition to formal classroom training, we conduct quarterly recurring training for counselors. The aim of these sessions is to highlight topical issues, update counselors on current procedures and get feedback from the "guys in the trenches." From time to time, the New Members ministry also sends out postcards with helpful tips and new information affecting their ministry.

Administering the program also requires an elaborate process of scheduling people to be present for duty at the various services. As you can imagine, three services and

50–60 people coming forward each weekend require a good deal of coordination. While your church may have fewer decisions each weekend, the basics of the program are probably just as appropriate for you. If you have a larger number of people coming forward from time to time (during special sermons and events, for instance), it is very helpful to have a coordinator who decides which counselor is paired up with which person who is coming forward. As the person coming forward is escorted back into the semiprivate counseling area, either Bob or Dave have a brief word of welcome and encouragement. Bob and Dave are good about prepping the people coming forward for this interview with words to the effect of: "whether you have been a Christian one day, or 30 years, we go through this information with everyone, because it is so important."

I hope the above narrative adequately depicts the seriousness we ascribe to the decision counseling process. Our intent is to gently and lovingly lead a person to a saving relationship with Jesus Christ while at the same time ensuring that people who are motivated by the wrong reasons or who aren't ready spiritually are given an opportunity for further growth before joining the church.

Part Three

MAKING YOUR CHURCH A PLACE TO SERVE

Chapter 9

Where to Start:
An Introduction

Every day they continued to meet together in the temple courts. They broke bread in their homes and ate together with glad and sincere hearts, praising God and enjoying the favor of all the people. And the Lord added to their number daily those who were being saved. Acts 2:46-47

I was working in the church's Facilities Department in 1998 when my boss, Brett DeYoung, Administrator of Education called me into his office to offer me a new position. During my 28-year career in the USAF I got a new job just about every year, so I was ready psychologically for a change, having administered the Facilities program for over three years. I can't say I was too disappointed about leaving a job that often dealt with stopped up toilets for one where I got to talk to people about Jesus.

Anyway, Brett explained the position in the following way. At that point Southeast was doing a great job of getting people into the church and helping them make a decision for Christ. Then, in Brett's words, "we baptize them, give them a Bible, and tell them to go get involved." While he was exaggerating just a bit, I took his point. This process is a great way to make new members, but it leaves something to be desired in the assimilation process. While we had done all right in converting spectators into participants because of the early and consistent emphasis from the pulpit, the congregation had grown too large to rely on this principle alone. A rational, logical process was required, and after much prayer, I was selected to take on this project.

Creating a process from scratch was a challenging, but important task for a couple of reasons. First, new members were streaming in the front door. We conducted a "Decision Weekend" in January 1999 two weeks after moving into our new facility and 160 joined the church. I joked that we should put a "Closed" sign on the front door until I could get caught up with the paperwork. I had seen lots of paperwork as a government bureaucrat, but the mounting piles of Decision Counseling forms were starting to remind me of my days in the Pentagon. Second, the church was at a critical juncture. We needed to attract and retain new converts if we were to sustain the phenomenal growth Southeast had experienced in the past. But from a broader perspective, the survival of the church of Jesus Christ in the 21st century depends on our ability to build up Christ's body here on earth. The imperative is great and the challenge to the survival of Christ's church on earth is enormous. As I began my research, I was struck by the challenge to the church today.

George Barna wrote in *The Second Coming of the Church*:

> The Church in America is losing influence and adherents faster than any other major institution in the nation. At the risk of sounding like an alarmist, I believe the Church in America has no more than five years — perhaps even less — to turn itself around and begin to affect the culture, rather than be affected by it.[11]

In his book, *Exit Interviews,* William Hendricks postulated that an estimated 53,000 people leave churches every week and never come back. He wrote:

> It is not enough for the church to attract new 'customers.' It must also hold onto the ones it has. Why? Because that's the purpose of the church — people

development. The church exists to "prepare God's people for works of service, so that the body of Christ may be built up until we all reach unity in the faith and the knowledge of the Son of God and become mature, attaining to the whole measure of the fullness of Christ."[12]

Thom Rainer in *High Expectations* found that, if members of a church only attend worship services, only 16% will still be attending in five years. If, however, they become an active part of a Sunday School, that percentage goes up to 83%.[13] Clearly there is an enormous imperative to attract and retain new Christians and to fully involve those who are already believers.

In Chapter 4 I reviewed the process we went through to develop the assimilation model and program we used. Regardless of the specific program you select, there are a number of essential prerequisites for any effective program.

PREREQUISITES FOR AN EFFECTIVE DISCIPLING PROGRAM

1. **Process is as important as content.** Each element of the process must be linked to the next. We have tried to be consistent in emphasizing the individual's next step. For instance, when the individual talks to a decision counselor, they are provided a card with a list of next step activities (Appendix 18). The decision counselor would review the options with the new member and write on the card, "Your next step is to attend *What We Believe*," for example. Everyone's next step is to attend *Welcome to Southeast!* At *Welcome to Southeast!* (which will be described later) we give the attendees a similar next step card and have them individually specify what their next step is. We have tried to indoctrinate the staff to emphasize the "next step" process any time they come in contact with a guest or new member.

2. **You need to communicate your program through the widest possible variety of media.** I conducted an informal sur-

vey of new members soon after we launched our program to determine how they had learned about *Welcome to Southeast!* I was hoping that one way would be most effective and we could confine our energies there. No such luck. I talked with a dozen people. Three saw the announcement in the bulletin. Four heard about it in the guest reception. Two read about it in the letter we sent them after they joined. Two read about it in *The Outlook*. One remembered that a Decision Counselor had mentioned it to them. What does this mean? It means you have to advertise your program in a multitude of ways. As described in Chapter 3, we send out lots of letters and make countless phone calls, in addition to bulletin notices, pulpit announcements, newsletter articles, decision counselors, guest services, etc.

3. I would also urge you to **consider the names of your programs very carefully.** They need to describe what the program is. I think we messed up here, and our program was initially less effective than it might have been. We selected "Life" as the theme of our assimilation program. *New Life*, was our spiritual gifts class; *Discover Life*, our basic Christianity course, and *Share Life* was to be our personal evangelism class. I joked that we need another class titled "Get a Life." But, the problem with these names was that they didn't describe what the course dealt with, and as a consequence, I believe, the classes were not as effective as they might otherwise have been. To the uninitiated, i.e., the people we were trying to reach, the names were arcane at best. What was "New Life" anyway? "Discover Your Spiritual Gifts" was much more descriptive. "Discover Life," too, didn't give the listener a feel for what the program content was. After the first year we changed *Discover Life* to *Basic Bible* and reverted to "Discover Your Spiritual Gifts" as the name of that class.

4. **Follow up, follow up, follow up.** It's not enough to develop a program; it takes tenacity, perseverance, and hard work to make it become a reality. You just have to keep after people when implementing a new program. You also need to

make sure facilities are scheduled, double check that refreshments are ordered, check room arrangements, and have a backup plan if your primary audio visual system fails. I know this sounds pretty pedestrian, but I cannot overemphasize the importance of following up to confirm all the details. It's about excellence, and excellence really matters when you're trying to make a good first impression.

A good example of the need for follow up was demonstrated in implementing the sponsor program, which in large measure depended on our ABF classes. Our 43 ABF classes are exceedingly busy, so implementing the sponsor program required continuous follow up until it became a standard practice. But getting the names of the ABF class coordinators for the program was so much like pulling teeth that our sponsor team felt they earned their Doctorates in Dentistry. I guess what I'm saying is that it's relatively easy to design a program but, as Ross Perot is fond of saying, "The Devil is in the details," and we want to minimize the Devil's involvement in our church programs, as much as possible.

5. You need to **carefully consider when to schedule your programs.** Your programs should be offered at different times: during the Sunday School hour, on weekends, and evenings as much as possible. While you want to offer choices, I recommend that you avoid multiple sessions whenever possible for new member, introductory programs. We have had little success with multiple sessions. For instance, we initially offered *Welcome to Southeast!* in two parts, and it was a better program in two sessions. Unfortunately, we discovered that less than 25 percent of the new members were attending both sessions. I asked a number of attendees why they were unable to attend both sessions and the responses were predictable. Work, family, and other obligations made it difficult to attend both sessions, and since *WTS!* was not a requirement for church membership (it was kind of regarded as "optional for extra credit"), it was the obligation that was crossed off the schedule first.

For these reasons we reduced it to a single session. It wasn't as comprehensive, but those attending received a better overall view of Southeast, I think. It really makes sense when you think about it. Our culture today demands options and a variety of choices. Additionally, given the pretty hectic scheduling of a normal family, we are better off limiting the number of times we interrupt the schedule of a new member. Later as a new member matures and their commitment to the church increases, we can make more demands on them. Just as a point of comparison, I have listed below the times we offer our classes. The content of these programs will be discussed later.

Program	*When Scheduled*
Welcome to Southeast!	ABF Hour: Saturday, 6:30 p.m.; Sunday, 9:15 a.m.
Basic Bible	Sunday, 9:15 a.m.
What We Believe	Sunday, 5:00–7:00 p.m. Sunday, 8:30–10:30 a.m. Wednesday, 7:00–9:00 p.m.
Spiritual Gifts Class	Saturday, 8:30–12:30 p.m.
Small Group Study of John	Sunday or Monday or Tuesday, 7:00–9:00 p.m.
Building Bridges	Friday, 7:00–9:00 p.m. Saturday, 9:00 a.m.–12:30 p.m.
Pizza with Preachers	Sunday, 5:00–7:00 p.m.

As we went to press, we were planning to implement a more coherent track system that will offer almost all classes on a trimester basis as depicted in the table below. We hope that this will provide a logical, easy-to-follow system for all New Member classes and other Bible studies.

Period \ Level	1st Trimester Sep–Nov (11 wk)	2nd Trimester Jan–Apr (13 wk)	3rd Trimester Jun–Aug (11 wk)
Level 3	Precepts Electives	Precepts Electives	Precepts Electives
Level 2	Experiencing God Building Bridges Electives**	Experiencing God Building Bridges Electives**	Experiencing God Building Bridges Electives**
Level 1	Bible 101/201* Spiritual Formation Electives Search for Significance	Bible 102/202* Walk Thru Bible Electives Search for Significance	Spiritual Formation Electives Search for Significance
Basic	Basic Bible Basic Christianity What We Believe	Basic Bible Basic Christianity What We Believe	Basic Bible Basic Christianity What We Believe

- Minimize effect of student's missing classes with handouts, reviews, and previews
- Conduct identical *Basic Bible* on Sunday at 9:15–10:45 and Monday at 7:00–8:30, 52 weeks a year (except Labor Day, Christmas, and Easter).

*101 — Genesis to Esther; 102 — Job–Song of Solomon; 201 — Prophets–Gospels; 202 — Acts–Revelation

**Defending Your Faith, Prayer, How to Study Your Bible, Countering Mormonism, etc.

Chart 9: Progressive Track System of Scheduling Bible Studies and Other Classes

6. **Let new members know what is expected of them.** In his book, *High Expectations,* Thom Rainer maintains that one of the keys, perhaps **the** key to success in effective churches, is that they set and communicate high expectations to their membership.[14] As I mentioned in the first chapter, I think Southeast did a really good job of setting high standards of excellence and communicating those standards to the congregation. As we grew, however, I don't think we were as intentional about articulating expectations of membership to new members. The message just got diluted by our greater numbers. For this reason we developed six expectations of Southeast members and made them a point of emphasis at our orientation program, *Welcome to Southeast!*

Over time, these expectations began to come up in other areas of the church as well.

Initially some resisted this feeling that perhaps the church was being a little too assertive. Resistance began to wane when we realized that there are expectations associated with being a member of any organization, and members don't resent, but rather appreciate, knowing what is expected of them. This just makes sense. When I joined the Air Force, there were certain expectations of membership in that group and those expectations were communicated to me very clearly. Matter of fact, if I violated those expectations, I might be punished under the Uniform Code of Military Justice (UCMJ). I proposed that for Southeast some years ago, but thus far the idea hasn't caught on. I mean, if we shot deserters, that might dissuade others from leaving for another church.

Expectations for Southeast Members

1. **Grow in your relationship with Christ.** That includes regular attendance at worship and other church activities. I'm sure this seems pretty obvious to most people who have been active in the church, but to many people new to the church this is not an expectation of church membership. We discovered to our disappointment that, when asked, a sizable number of people said they responded to the invitation because "they wanted to be a member of Southeast." The "more perfect" answer is to have a personal relationship with Jesus Christ or to mature in that relationship.

2. **Live a life that honors God and Southeast.** Every church member is a potential hypocrite, and our critics are just waiting to point out when a Christian doesn't represent his or her faith very well. We expect our members to live on Monday through Friday the way they worship on the weekend. The illustration I use involves the "Southeast" bumper sticker that adorns my 1990 Honda. I've never been a "bumper sticker" kind of guy, but when my wife and I

moved back to Louisville, my mother gave me one and I dutifully put the Southeast Christian Church bumper sticker on my rear bumper.

Now after flying supersonic fighter jets for a quarter of a century, I occasionally forget that the Honda is not an F-15, and I exceed the speed limit a tad or drive aggressively as if I still lived in Germany. Do you think that bumper sticker has a restraining influence on the way I drive? Of course it does. While I'm not perfect (just forgiven as the cliché goes), I am conscious that when I drive, I represent Southeast on the highways. For that reason, I am more restrained than I might otherwise be. I suggest we should live our lives as if we had a bumper sticker with the name of our church stuck to our forehead, or better yet like we wear the name of Jesus.

3. **Get involved in a small group.** There are quite a few people who are content to remain anonymous and get lost in the crowd. Unfortunately, they miss so much of what a large church has to offer both spiritually and socially. For this reason we encourage everyone to get involved in a small group and we try to make that easy for them.

4. **Get involved in a ministry.** As detailed earlier, this has been an expectation of membership from the very beginning, and we hope people will be motivated to become participants in the work God is doing here at Southeast, not out of a sense of duty but rather because it is exciting and rewarding to be part of a church that does things with excellence.

5. **Give regularly.** Southeast has been richly blessed financially despite the fact that the subject is rarely mentioned from the pulpit. Generally, there are about two sermons a year on the subject of giving but no weekly appeals to dig deeper. Surprisingly, our people have been so generous that in 1999, Bob Russell publicly applauded their generosity. That was a first for me — a preacher congratulating a congregation for their generosity.

6. **Help Southeast grow.** We emphasize that we aren't seeking numbers for number's sake, but we want to grow so

that the body of Christ may be built up and the gospel shared with more people in the community.

As you develop your program and define your process of assimilating new members, I suggest you keep these general principles in mind and that you integrate membership expectations in all of your programs. You need a clear, logical process built upon solid foundational principles. If you refer back to our assimilation model, you'll notice that the first step in our assimilation process is "Connecting" new members.

Chapter 10

Connecting New Members: The Assimilation Process Begins

The first thing Andrew did was to find his brother Simon and tell him, "We have found the Messiah" (that is, the Christ). And he brought him to Jesus.

Jesus looked at him and said, "You are Simon son of John. You will be called Cephas" (which, when translated, is Peter).

John 1:41-42

Once a person has become a member, the assimilation process begins, and the first step is to make people feel part of the organization. We call this process "connecting," and it means that a new member has been contacted personally, they have at least one person they can call a friend, and they know what their next step is to get more fully involved in the church.

While this is a critical step in the process, I can't say we were very effective initially. We were having about 200 people a month join Southeast, but connecting with each one was a hit and miss operation. The decision counseling session was great for leading someone to Christ or for making them a member, but it didn't always contribute to connecting a new member to the church. As mentioned earlier, the time with a decision counselor was brief, and for many it was a stressful occasion where matters of a deeply personal and spiritual nature were discussed. For these reasons, decision counselors couldn't realistically communicate much in the way of substantive information on how to get involved in Southeast ministries.

At the beginning we really didn't have a comprehensive, high touch, follow-up program after a person became a member. The individual decision counselor was expected to contact the people they had counseled the next week and follow-up periodically afterwards. In reality, this didn't happen on a consistent basis. Despite their best intentions, volunteer decision counselors had other things to do and the stack of new members needing to be contacted grew as time passed.

As a result, we missed involvement opportunities. We hoped we could compensate for missed connecting opportunities by inviting new members and guests to attend *Welcome to Southeast!* our orientation program which I will discuss shortly. Unfortunately, only 18% of all new members elected to attend *WTS!* I attribute this situation to three factors. One, due to the vast number of programs offered by the church, new members viewed *Welcome to Southeast!* as another program instead of the main entry point to other church programs. Basically, we just weren't getting the attention of a sizeable number of new members despite the carefully designed program of bulletin announcements, letters, reminder cards, and phone calls.

Correcting this situation involved time to indoctrinate the staff, leadership, and the congregation to the new way of doing business. We needed to "institutionalize" the process to make *Welcome to Southeast!* as much of the normal Southeast routine as worship, small groups, and ABF. Ideally, after a Southeast member first encountered a guest or new member the first words out of their mouth needed to be, "Welcome. You need to attend *Welcome to Southeast!*" We are still struggling to educate everyone, but these things take time and determination. Remember principle number 4? Follow up, follow up, follow up.

I didn't discover the second reason for low *Welcome to Southeast!* attendance until a year after we launched the program. I had always assumed that a new member was, well, a new member. In January 2000 we discovered that while all of our new members were new to membership, they weren't new to Southeast and for that reason they didn't feel compelled to attend *Welcome to Southeast!* As I mentioned earlier, the median time between first attending and joining was 18 months, and many had put off joining for five years or more. Understandably, these people did not feel like they needed to attend an orientation course. As a matter of fact, most of them could probably teach the course as they had been attending longer than some of our deacons. We're presently evaluating new ways to help the "old" new members identify their "next step," and we think it may be the spiritual gifts program.

A third problem we experienced was that, initially, the new member was essentially left on their own to attend the introduction to Southeast. Many churches make the initial orientation class mandatory and offer it during the worship and Sunday School hours. At my son's church in Florida, he and his wife had to take a three-hour orientation course before they were accepted into membership. Since they missed worship services during the class they were given a tape of the sermon to take with them.

There's no consistent practice among churches. During a Leadership Network conference (involving a wide variety of denominations) I conducted an informal poll of attendees to see how many churches required the program for membership. Of the 10 people sitting at my table, five had an orientation program and three required it for membership. At Southeast's Fall 1999 Leadership Conference (the vast majority of attendees are independent Christian Church members), I conducted a more extensive survey. We had 42 churches respond to the survey. Only 17 had an orientation program, and none required it for membership. Thom

Rainer found that of the churches he surveyed, all but 27 percent had programs and 18 percent required these programs for membership.[15]

We have not elected to make the orientation program mandatory for membership as it would be inconsistent with our values and past experience. We don't want anything to interfere with a person joining the church or attending worship. Since our membership requirements have served us well, I had no inclination to add another requirement to the process. At the same time we must recognize that new members who don't participate in our orientation program will be less committed and in some cases less mature spiritually if they aren't provided a sound indoctrination at the very beginning.

NEW MEMBER SPONSOR PROGRAM

To help resolve these problems, we implemented a New Member Sponsor program the second year. I got this idea from Frazier Memorial Church in Montgomery, Alabama, who called their initiative the "Buddy Program."

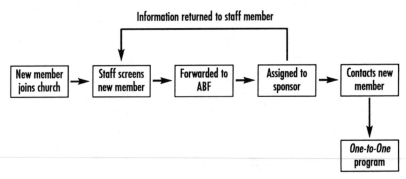

Chart 10: The New Member Sponsor Process

New Member Sponsor Program Process

1. When someone joins the church, the Decision Counselor explains the program to the new member and advises him or her that a sponsor will be contacting them soon.

2. As part of joining the church, new members provide us a good deal of personal information on the decision counseling sheet. As the New Member ministry receives the new member paper work, we match the individual to an ABF class consistent with their age, marital status, and worship service they attend. (Appendix 19 contains our forms for tracking the sponsor program.)

3. The new member's decision counseling sheet (Appendix 31) and detailed instructions are forwarded to an ABF class with a brightly colored cover sheet for ease of identification. Each ABF class has a new member coordinator who assigns the new member to a member of the ABF class for sponsoring. The New Member Sponsor's responsibilities are to:

a. Pray for the person they are sponsoring.

b. Invite them to their ABF class. They are also expected to encourage them to attend other ABF classes to find the right fit.

c. Make at least one contact with the new member each month for six months to a year and advise them of church activities that might be of interest to them.

d. Encourage them to attend *Welcome to Southeast!*, *What We Believe*, and other new member events.

e. Be alert for people who might want to establish a deeper discipleship relationship by participating in the *One-to-One* ministry (explained later).

f. Invite them out to lunch or into their home for a meal. We also provide a free ticket for the sponsor to take the new member and their families to our Wednesday evening fellowship meal prior to our Celebration Worship and Praise Service dinner.

g. Essentially, we ask that our New Member Sponsors be a Christian friend to the new member, take them by the hand, and help them take full advantage of all Southeast has to offer.

Implementing this program was an enormous challenge, and we still have a way to go. (We used our ABFs as an initial resource pool to kick off the program, but our long-term vision was to identify a pool of several hundred sponsors for our new members.) Our ABF classes initially weren't enthusiastic about the program since they were already heavily involved in church activities, and this was one more thing we were asking them to do. Still the program worked to the mutual benefit of both the class and the church. The church benefited by another new member connection opportunity and the class got another potential member.

IMPLEMENTING THE PROGRAM

Planning for the program began four months before implementation on January 1, 2000. We implemented the program using the following steps:

1. The Director of Education signed a letter (Appendix 20) to each teacher and class leader announcing the program and explaining the program details. Since sponsorship falls in the general category of discipleship, we developed a discipleship lesson for presentation to all ABF classes during a three-month period before implementing the program. The lesson was available for the ABF teacher to present, or my boss or I would visit the class to present the material. The objective was to help ABF class members understand the need for being disciples and to explain the details of how they could become disciplers by becoming involved in the sponsor program. In the end, Greg and I taught about a dozen of the classes. (Appendix 21 contains the lesson plan for this class.)

2. One month out I sent a letter to remind the class leaders that the program would begin the next month and asked them to identify a class coordinator for the program. The organization was a key factor and is depicted in the accompanying chart.

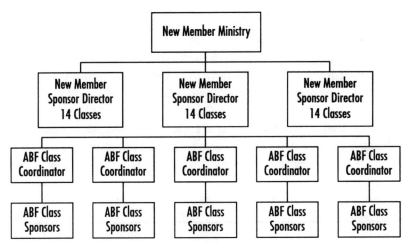

Chart 11: Sponsorship Organization

3. I wrote an article describing the program in our weekly newspaper, *The Outlook.*

4. During the first week in January, we received the first batch of decision counseling forms and sent each one to the class coordinator. The packages were easily identified by the brightly colored cover sheets and contained four items (See Appendix 19):

 a. A set of instructions that explained exactly what the sponsor was supposed to do.

 b. The decision counseling sheet.

 c. A new member commitment form that identified who was to sponsor the new member. The form was returned to the new member secretary so we could keep track of who was sponsoring whom.

 d. A sheet for keeping track of contacts made with the new member. At the end of six months the sheet was to be returned to the New Member ministry indicating contacts made and whether or not the new member got plugged in to church activities.

5. The New Member support staff kept track of all these actions on a computer spreadsheet that was provided to the directors on a weekly basis.

6. Two months into the program we were getting returned confirmation on about one-third of the new members assigned to sponsors. After visiting many of the classes, I am confident many more new members were being contacted by their sponsors, but the paper trail was not being completed. At this point **we sent out letters of encouragement to the classes that contained a "report card" on how each class was doing.** The directors then went to their respective classes and gave a little pep talk on how important the program was and encouraged the coordinators and new member sponsors to be conscientious about contacting their sponsorees.

I was not so naïve as to believe the program would be readily accepted without a significant followup effort. It was hard work. This is where a core group of three impassioned volunteers was critical. Ken Mudd, John Schmitt, and Bill Williams (two of whom were new members themselves) formed the nucleus of the implementation efforts. They had about a dozen or so ABF classes to oversee. In this capacity they had regular contact with the coordinators and specific new member sponsors. Their goal was to hold sponsors accountable to ensure contact was being made and to assist in any way necessary. These guys spent countless hours on the phone prodding, cajoling, and motivating class coordinators and sponsors to commit to the program. To be honest this program wasn't effective using ABF classes to implement it and we are now relying on our small groups ministry. Still, I think it is a solid program that may work well at your church.

ONE-TO-ONE

Everyone needs to have a friend at church, and that's what we hoped to achieve with the sponsor program. But many new members need more; they need to be discipled. These new members were either new to the faith or not very mature in their walk with Christ. To address this need, the New Member program was fortunate to inherit an already established program that began some years before with the goal of helping new people grow in their relationship with Christ on an individual basis.

The program provides a structured way to grow in Christ by establishing a close one-on-one studying relationship with another believer. A more mature Christian, the "discipler," is matched with a newer or less-studied Christian called a "disciple."

The *One-to-One* program is administered almost exclusively by volunteers and uses the Christian Businessmen's *Operation Timothy Studies* as curriculum. The discipler and disciplee go through four books, usually in meetings that last from an hour to an hour and a half.

I wish I could say that hundreds of people availed themselves of this wonderful opportunity, but in reality the number of people in the program was only 25-40, with more women than men participating. Nevertheless, the ones who were involved were enthusiastic about the positive impact the program had on their lives.

One of those success stories is about a new member named Larry. Larry grew up in Louisville and considered a number of professional options before buying a bar which was known for its party atmosphere. Larry, too, was very much a part of the party scene indulging in alcohol, drugs, and other worldly pleasures. He ridiculed people who lived more conventional life styles, and shunned religion.

His road to a personal relationship with Jesus Christ began indirectly when he looked around his bar one evening and viewed the lives of his patrons. He didn't like what he saw. Worse yet, it occurred to him that he was very much like they were — headed nowhere. In 1994, Larry enrolled in AA and NA and now has been sober for 5 years. In these programs he made a commitment to "step three" of the AA 12-step process and made a decision to turn his will and life over to God. Larry described it as his "pre-Altar call."

Sometime later, a friend recommended that Larry attend a revival in Florida, but Larry opted to take a fishing trip to New York. As "luck" would have it, his plans changed, and Larry unexpectedly ended up in Florida and elected to attend the revival. There he had a profound spiritual experience. Since then he has joined Southeast and involved himself in an ABF, Bible Studies and other activities. He has benefited enormously from the *One-to-One* program with a Southeast member named Roger. Larry credits *One-to-One* with providing indispensable assistance as he attempted to build upon his conversion experience and grow in his relationship with Christ.

WELCOME TO SOUTHEAST!

The centerpiece of the Involvement program, *Welcome to Southeast!*, provides an overview of Southeast beliefs, activities, and church organization. Because we are a big church, we can offer an impressive number of programs and activities, but the sheer number of these programs can be bewildering and actually represent an obstacle to becoming involved. For that reason *WTS!* introduces our guests and new members to the 20 or so separate ministries available here.

As previously mentioned, we initially fielded the program as two, one-hour sessions held on different dates. The first session talked about Southeast as a place to "Grow," and the second as a place to "Serve." Session one described the involvement model, gave a brief history of the church, a condensed outline of church beliefs, and suggested some ways the new members could grow in their relationship with Christ. The second session dealt with church organization, membership expectations, and ministry opportunities.

We conducted a "mini-ministry" fair after the second *Welcome to Southeast!* session that was very helpful to new members. During the fair, representatives of each ministry manned simple booths and answered questions and recruited new members. When the number of people attending *WTS!* was over a hundred per month, the ministry fair was a great idea. When attendance slipped to 35-50 per session, it became impractical, and we deleted the fair as part of the program. However, Southeast normally conducts elaborate ministry fairs in conjunction with our semi-annual leadership conferences, and we sought to use these events to expose new members to ministry opportunities by inviting them to attend.

At the end of each *WTS!* session we spend about 15 minutes in fellowship circles to get to know each other better. Being a task-oriented person, I wasn't too enthusiastic about the relational aspect of the sessions, but learned eventually how essential they are. **If you're going to hold on to new members, it is essential that you give your people every opportunity to develop friendships** and identify their next step in the assimilation process.

Our *WTS!* fellowship circles consisted of 6-8 new members with a deacon or new member volunteer as a part of each group to facilitate the discussion. The leader went first to model the correct way to participate. Then, each person introduced themselves, briefly discussed their family, hobbies, and where they were born. They shared their religious background and told the group why they first attended Southeast.

Over time, the fellowship circles became my favorite part of the program. Not only did I enjoy listening to their stories, but I marveled at the relationships that were formed. I recall one incident in particular. A middle-aged woman was elaborating on her childhood growing up in Louisville's west end. She talked about her family, the neighborhood where she had grown up, and the school she attended. A lady sitting across the circle was intensely interested and finally couldn't contain herself. "Your mother used to cut my hair! We grew up together!" Sure enough, these two ladies had been friends many years before but hadn't seen each other in over 30 years. It was fun watching them renew old relationships.

As these groups evolved, we added one important step. As each person talked about themselves, they were encouraged to conclude by identifying their next step. We provided a card (Appendix 18) that listed all programs relevant to new members. These had been explained during the briefing. New members speculated about what their specific next step would be and then wrote it down on the card, "My next step is . . ." These cards were collected, the person's name entered on a roster, and followup reminder cards were sent before the next class was conducted.

As I discussed in Chapter 9, after two months' experience conducting *WTS!* we discovered that less than 25% of *WTS!* attendees were showing up for both sessions, and we concluded that the program should be consolidated into a single session. This was no easy task since we were trying to cram so much material into the program already. Initially, I tried talking faster and soon began to sound like Alvin the Chipmunk or that fast talking guy in the old Fed Ex commercials. Nevertheless, by deleting some material totally and abbreviating other parts, we were able to present a clear briefing that addressed the basics of Southeast.

Appendix 23 contains copies of the slides we use for the *WTS!* briefing. These slides are generic but you can give your presentation some pizzazz by adding pictures and colorful stories. The agenda is:

1. Introduction
2. Describe the process for involvement. The "wheel" diagram.
3. Review history — a three-minute video was shown in conjunction with history
4. What we believe
5. Mission statement (see Chapter 1)
6. How to grow spiritually — daily devotions, prayer, Bible study, worship, and fellowship
7. Review church organization — elders, deacons, staff

8. Membership expectations
9. Ministries described
10. Fellowship circles.

The format of the *WTS!* presentation was important. Southeast has committed itself to doing things in an excellent manner, so we wanted a first-class presentation. This was particularly important as the program was one of the first small group experiences for guests and new members. For these reasons we procured a video projector, computer, and VCR to enable us to present a Power Point presentation with attractive slides. All this was designed to create a positive image of excellence that would make the participants want to get more involved.

We also produced an attractive notebook with multicolor cover to be given to each attendee. (Appendix 24 contains the *Welcome to Southeast!* Notetaker.) Other churches' notebooks are smaller (about the size of a Bible) and are very professional looking. Some churches have the sermon notetaker printed on the same sized paper with holes punched that allow insertion into the binder. I hope we can upgrade to this format in the future, but in the developmental stages an 8 ½ x 11 format reproduced on the office copier was fine and saved a lot of money as we continually made changes to the printed material while we learned what we were doing. The three-ring binder contained a notetaker for the presentation and tabs for additional information. We hoped the notebook would become a single source document for new members containing a yearly schedule, important church phone numbers, prayer and devotional study aids, and blank tabs for insertion of other new member materials provided at other programs.

There are a number of administrative details to consider before launching your first orientation program. Signage and room location are not insignificant considerations. The people coming to a new member function will generally be unfamiliar with your facility. Make sure signs clearly identify where the function is to be held. Likewise, make sure the room is conveniently located so new members can find it easily. We began with a room location very near the sanctuary, which was ideal. Later, however, the orientation program was moved up to the second floor. Not only did participation decline but the prominence of the program in people's minds was diminished as well. We're planning on moving back to our original location.

Should you have people register for *WTS!* and other programs? We do not. While it is helpful to anticipate how many will attend, we didn't want anything to discourage people from attending. We do ask that they call our hotline "so we can have materials available." For other programs, we ask people to register but don't insist that they do. Our experience is that 25% of people who register don't show up and about 10–15% of the attendees just drop in. So, unless meals are being served, there is no particular advantage to having people register.

When *WTS!* participants arrive, they should be able to sign in and get a name tag and a notebook quickly and efficiently. Nametags are essential. We use Microsoft Word labels program and overprint 2 × 4 inch labels with the Southeast church logo to make an attractive and inexpensive nametag. Initially we prepared preprinted name tags for those who registered, but the 25% no-show rate made that impractical. Remember to provide pens with thick black tips so the names are easy to read. A sign-in roster is also important for followup contacts and assessing how many new members are attending your sessions. Once the new members and guests are signed in, they can obtain refreshments and chat with the church members whom you have arranged to be there.

Tours of the facility should be offered. Existing members take this requirement for granted since we are familiar with the church, but new members may be totally unfamiliar with less public areas of the church. Since *WTS!* takes place during church hours when the building is crowded, tours at that time are impractical. We now offer tours in conjunction with the Sunday evening New Member get-together called "Pizza with the Preachers," which will be discussed later.

When do you offer the orientation program? We offer it during the ABF hours: 6:30 on Saturday evening and 9:15 a.m. on Sunday. This is convenient since child care is available and the session doesn't require a special trip to church. Popular times for other churches are Sunday evening or Saturday morning. We anticipate changing to the 11:00 hour on Sunday so we can benefit from the pulpit announcement at the 9:15 service. The reminder from the pulpit at the service preceding *WTS!* makes a big difference in attendance.

At the beginning of our *WTS!* program we developed a "slick," attractive, four-color brochure to advertise the program, provide some information about the church, and allow new members to sign up for various programs and ministry positions. A copy of the brochure appears in Appendix 22. Unfortunately, the slick variety was very expensive and, to be honest, we weren't getting a lot of them returned by new members. For that reason we went to a two-color, similar design which serves the intended purpose, but with dramatically less cost.

In conducting the WTS! program we make extensive use of New Member deacons and volunteers in an administrative capacity. They help set up, sign people in, and participate in the fellowship groups at the end. Initially, I presented the briefing that constituted the majority of the session, about 45 minutes. While I really enjoyed doing this, it has long been Southeast's policy to empower our lay leadership in all of our programming. In addition, plugging people into ministries is the purpose of an effective assimilation program. For these reasons, we began handing off the teaching duties to talented lay leaders. One deacon, Charles McKibben, took over most of the responsibility for *Welcome to Southeast!*

not only presenting the briefing but making substantive improvements to what was presented. Another deacon, Tony Ford taught *Discover Life*, our basics-of-Christianity class and later got involved with our *Basic Bible* course. If I had it to do over again, I would involve these talented lay leaders earlier in the process.

NEW MEMBER GET-TOGETHER

In August of 1999 I attended an evangelism conference at Willow Creek. At one of the sessions, I sat at a table with two ladies from our sister church in Lexington, Kentucky, Southland Christian Church. We struck up an interesting and productive conversation about assimilation programs and agreed it was more than a little ironic that while we only worked an hour from each other we had to travel to the outskirts of Chicago to exchange information about our programs. For that reason we resolved to get together in the near future, which we did in October 1999.

While Southland had many programs that interested us, one in particular met our needs the best. We were looking for another way to connect guests and new members to the church and have them come in contact with Bob and Dave. Southland conducts periodic pizza parties for new members. They invite new members to come to the church for pizza on a Wednesday evening and to participate in a brief, but informative program. A key feature is the appearance of their senior minister who gives the new members a pep talk about Southland's mission and values.

In 2000, we decided to do something similar. We had about 2800 people who had come forward since we moved into our new building. We invited 1,000 of them to our first new member get-together by sending out postcards. After considerable discussion and hand wringing over what to name the event, we called it "Pizza with the Preachers" and planned to conduct the get-together quarterly. We wanted to keep the format informal and offer the maximum opportunity for new members to come in contact with the staff and with each other.

Our associate minister Dave Stone, who has a keen wit, led things off with a spirited welcome peppered with humor and good cheer. We then had a simple icebreaker for about 15 minutes at each table. Individuals were encouraged to spend a few minutes answering specific questions about themselves and to idenify the newest new member (the one who had joined most recently) and the new member who had been attending the longest before joining. It is instructive to note that the newest new member had become a member only three weeks prior to the event. Interestingly, we had two people at our first affair who attended Southeast for 14 years before they took the step of membership. We offered prizes to the oldest and newest new members.

After the icebreaker, we ate pizza for 30 minutes. I conducted a panel discussion with three people who were involved in the church. Bob closed the formal part of the evening by talking about Southeast's mission, vision, and membership expectations. Everyone was invited to attend *WTS!* and to get involved in our ministries so they can serve Christ better and also be a larger part of the exciting work God is doing at Southeast. Again, there was ample opportunity for new members to meet others and form new relationships. We offered tours of the facility afterward. Overall, I think this undertaking was an enormous success.

Chapter 11

Helping New Members Grow to Christlike Maturity

Instead, speaking the truth in love, we will in all things grow up into him who is the Head, that is, Christ. From him the whole body, joined and held together by every supporting ligament, grows and builds itself up in love, as each part does its work.

Ephesians 4:15,16

Once a new member is connected in some manner either by interaction with their sponsor or by attending *Welcome to Southeast!* the next step is to help them grow in their relationship with Christ and with Southeast. The emphasis in this case is fourfold:

1. **The new member should get involved in the Word.** A common thread among many, perhaps the majority of new members, is a limited knowledge of God's word. Those of us who have grown up in the church take a lot for granted. We assume everyone is fluent in Greek, knows the difference between pre- and postmillennialism and can find the book of Moses without looking in the table of contents. But a large proportion of our new members know very little about the Bible and even less about the essentials of our faith. This point was driven home to me in Spring of 1999 when I was teaching our first new member small group Bible study.

The initial class was compressed since we got a late

start in the quarter. I was teaching my heart out and trying to be as basic as possible but I knew, and explained to the class, that we were cramming a lot into a short period of time. Not content with my explanation, one of the participants wrote a thoughtful, but critical anonymous letter to Bob Russell complaining that we were "missing the mark." I hope he didn't mean *hamartia* which is Greek for "missing the mark," or "sin." He suggested that we provide a class called "The Bible for Dummies," a takeoff on the computer training books by a similar name. I took his point and early in the next year we began a *Basic Bible* course which lasted 13 weeks and provided a brief, general survey of the entire Bible emphasizing the overall organization, the general content of each book and the primary characters involved in the Old and New Testament and a dozen or so themes.

BASIC BIBLE

Basic Bible proved to be an effective and popular class. Appendix 25 contains the lesson plans. New Christians and older Christians who had neglected their Bible over the years, came to the class eager to learn about God's word. They were hungry for the gospel, asked difficult questions, and gobbled up every handout I could generate. In talking to these students, it quickly became clear that another class was needed, one that built upon the foundation *Basic Bible* laid. For this reason, we began to develop a series of classes that focused on specific books or categories of books in the Bible. Surprisingly, many of the *Basic Bible* students were not interested in ABFs. They felt little need for the "F" or fellowship and only wanted Bible Study.

OTHER BIBLE STUDIES

We stressed that new members should get involved in one of the numerous Bible studies offered by the various ministries. This, too, was easier said than done due to the bewildering array of offerings available for the new member to choose from. We could barely keep up with each new class; how could we expect a new member to figure it out? For this reason the Adult Ministries Department published a wonderful booklet of available Bible studies. This booklet was comprehensive, detailing every class offered, and it proved to be extremely helpful to new and existing members.

2. **The new member needs to get involved in a small group and/or ABF.** In his book, *High Expectations,* Thom Rainer pointed out the importance of Sunday School in retaining members. He found that people who became regular attendees to Sunday School remained as members. As previously noted, of those who didn't, all but 16% left the church within five years. In his study of "successful" churches he found that up to 55% of people in worship are involved in Sunday School. He went on to conclude that: "Sunday School is the most effective assimilation methodology in evangelistic churches today."[16] I agree! However we haven't yet been as successful as I would like in getting people plugged into an ABF class. Presently, our ABF attendance is about 2500 or about 15% of our membership. When you factor in irregular attenders the total may be close to 25%, and we're seeking ways to increase this number.

I'm not sure Sunday School attendance alone is a fair measure of involvement. When you consider the number of people in our robust small group program and others taking one of the numerous Bible studies, involved in accountability groups, or participating in other Bible-focused groups, the number is probably in the vicinity of Rainer's 55%. As a matter of fact, as discussed later in Chapter 15, our survey of new members revealed that 57% of them were participating in ABF, a small group, or volunteering in a ministry. I know these are apples-and-oranges comparisons, but unfortunately no standard, consistent measurements exist that I know of.

To get involved in an ABF, we recommended that everyone review the 40 or so classes and select three that match their age, marital status, and take place at a time compatible with their worship time. Many factors contribute to the decision as to which class to attend. Teaching is one factor, but fellowship and general chemistry are also important.

When my wife, Nancy, and I returned to Southeast after I retired from the Air Force, I didn't think we'd ever decide on a specific class. We attended 10 and liked them all. The teaching was uniformly good, and the classes were friendly for the most part. Ultimately, circumstances made the decision for us when I was asked to teach an ABF class. I can say without reservation that my association with this group of believers has been the best thing that has happened to me since I returned to Southeast.

SMALL GROUPS

Small groups are the lifeblood of a megachurch, but they can add spiritual depth and enhance the fellowship of any size church. For this reason we harp on small group involvement. When I say "small group," our Small Groups Minister, Murphy Belding, has taught me to include more than Home Bible Fellowship Groups. While I think small group Bible studies in homes is the most important part of a small groups ministry, any place that a member can experience community and spiritual service is a meaningful small group experience. We encourage groups of ushers, for instance, to gather for prayer before they serve and to share prayer requests to foster a sense of community and identity. Likewise, we encourage small group interaction in all of our Bible studies, even those that last only a limited period of time.

But unfortunately, some of the already established small groups are not easy to break into. I hate this, but I also understand that these groups were all but full and most are comfortable with their current composition. This is understandable since we encourage them to bond into an intimate group, and we shouldn't be surprised if they don't want to split up. In addition, groups that were open to new members weren't necessarily conveniently located in the community to allow new member attendance.

For these reasons we worked with the Small Group Ministry to inaugurate a new member study of John with a twofold purpose. One was to provide a basic Bible study and the second purpose was to form at least one new small group from each class. Two friends, Dick and Connie Wharton, had been successfully conducting a similar program for a while and they were instrumental in getting the program off the ground. Murphy experimented by offering this class at different times: Tuesday evening, Sunday evening, during the ABF hour, and Monday evening. Initially, 40-50 people showed up, and over time attendance settled into the 30s. Out of these 13-week sessions we developed a wonderful Bible Study, but I don't know that we were able to form any small groups from the specific classes. I do believe a significant number liked the experience, however, and made their way into a Home Bible Fellowship or similar group.

To further facilitate small group involvement we fielded new small groups whenever possible. Two examples are illustrative.

Pilot's Wives Fellowship Group

During a session of *Discover Life*, one of the participants, Pam Luette, expressed a need for some help in dealing with the stress of being a pilot's wife. She was married to a UPS pilot who was often away. Since I had flown jets in the Air Force for 25 years, my wife and I could relate to Pam's situation. It can be tough being married to a pilot with the frequent absences. Pam's husband, Glen, had been in the Air Force until he got out to fly for UPS. As Pam and I talked, it occurred to us that the Air Force has a good system for helping each other out and in dealing with these unique challenges, but it's a different situation in the civilian world.

As result of Pam's and my conversation, I contacted Lisa Winburn, a former Air Force officer married to a pilot. I had flown with Lisa's husband Jim while we were stationed together in Florida. Lisa agreed to make contact with Pam to see if she could help. Afterward we thought there might be some merit in creating a Pilot's Wives Fellowship group where people like Pam can meet others in similar circumstances. Our pilot's wives group has been quite successful. (I was the only male member of the group. As such I took the blame for any man- or flying-related problems.) Not only have we continued to meet periodically and discuss concerns of mutual interest, but we have created a caring group where spiritual, emotional, and fellowship needs can be met. Initially launched as a support group, the group was recast as a small group after a year to emphasize the fellowship aspect of our get-togethers.

Multiple Sclerosis Support Group

Another example of creating small groups to meet specific needs is our Multiple Sclerosis support group. My wife, Nancy, has had MS since she was a teenager. Due to the nature of the disease, we didn't get a definitive diagnosis until she was 42. Since that time we have dealt with Nancy's MS and have come in contact with many people suffering from more severe cases than Nancy's.

When we arrived at Southeast, we came in contact with a number of other people with the disease, and Nancy thought an MS Support Group would be helpful. For that reason, she began a support group in 1995 that has grown and flourished over the years. Not only do we minister to our own members, but nonmembers come to Southeast to participate in our program and hear the gospel in addition to information on how to contend with this debilitating disease.

3. **The new member needs to get involved in new member classes.** We offer two classes specifically designed for new members. The first is *What We Believe*. Bob Russell has taught this class for many years, and it has become a key component of our new member program. Initially, the program consisted of three two-hour sessions which covered the topics "Nine Essentials of an Evangelical Church," "What Is Christianity All About?" "How Reliable Is the Bible?" "Understanding Our Heritage," "What the Bible Teaches about Communion and Baptism," and "What the Church Ought to Be." In the past, the last session included a meal where members of the ministerial staff were present. However, when we moved into our new building and included some of the *What We Believe* information in other programs, the course was reduced to two, two-hour sessions and the meal was deleted.

Still the class is very effective. The truth of the gospel was shared by the senior pastor in an effective and entertaining manner. Invariably the number of decisions increased at the weekend services following *What We Believe*. We began making Decision Counselors available following *What We Believe,* and a number of people made decisions for Christ.

DISCOVER LIFE

Another class we offered was called "Discover Life." This was really an excellent class that, in four sessions, covered the basics of Christianity. The purpose was to help a seeker become a believer, and to help believers deepen their faith. The notetaker for this class is included in Appendix 26. The four sessions are: Session 1: Who Is God? Session 2: God's Plan for You and Me; Session 3: Who Is Jesus Christ? Session 4: What Does God Expect from Me? Unfortunately, for reasons I never fully understood *Discover Life* never took off, and we ultimately ceased offering it. I'm looking for another time slot and opportunity to offer this class again after repackaging it as "Basic Christianity."

4. **The final component of our program to help new members (and existing members as well) grow in their relationship with Christ is** *Discover Your Spiritual Gifts.* This class was instituted in 1992 by New Member Minister Les Hughes. It came in response to our awareness that we were not doing a great job of helping our congregation a) understand their spiritual gifts and b) learn how to use them in the advancement of God's kingdom here on earth. There are many useful programs available. Leadership Network's Starter Kit is good. Bruce Bugbee, who helped Willow Creek develop their Network program, has a program you can use. I really like the one we developed that is included in Appendix 27. (Though called "New Life," it is fundamentally the same as our *Discover Your Spiritual Gifts* class.)

We conduct this program on Saturday morning every other month from 8:30 to 12:30. It is an interesting, informative, and convicting program. The program consists of four parts.

1) The first deals with the biblical basis for spiritual gifts: what they are and why we have them.

2) The second part begins with a test that reveals the individual's spiritual gifts. Different spiritual gifts programs contain different gifts and groupings of gifts. All basically have their origin in 1 Corinthians 12. We divide ours into two broad categories (these are explained in the attachment):

Dynamic	Supporting
1. Encouragement	1. Administration
2. Giving	2. Discernment
3. Leadership	3. Evangelism
4. Mercy	4. Faith
5. Prophecy	5. Helping
6. Service	6. Knowledge
7. Teaching	7. Shepherding
	8. Wisdom

3) The third hour covers the role temperament and personality play in serving God. We use Florence Littauer's "Personality Plus" assessment tool. I first came in contact with these sorts of personality inventory tools in the Air Force and taught the Meyer Briggs Typology Indicator (MBTI) at Air War College. The awareness of the role our God-given temperament plays in our day-to-day lives has had a profound influence on me and my family. Before I became aware of my temperament and the temperament of others, I just assumed that I was the standard and everyone needed to be like me. However, when I discovered that there are four different temperaments each with its own strengths and weaknesses, it was very liberating. I began to appreciate the strengths of my wife and children; and became aware of my own weaknesses. This awareness has enormous potential for improving interpersonal relations at home, work, and church.

4) The final section of *Discover Your Spiritual Gifts* helps the students discover their passion and talents.

These four activities — Bible study, small groups, new member classes, and *Discover Your Spiritual Gifts* — form the foundation of our program to help new members grow to Christlike maturity. As they grow, they become ready to serve God by seeking out service opportunities at Southeast.

Chapter 12

From Growing to Serving ...
the Southeast Way

Do not merely listen to the word, and so deceive yourselves.
Do what it says.   James 1:22

Clearly Christ calls us to have a relationship with Him, to connect with Him and His body. He wants us to grow and mature in our Christian walk. But Jesus also expects us to do something with the gift of salvation and the spiritual gifts God has given us. The Bible teaches that we are to serve Him as part of the body of Christ, and at Southeast we emphasize serving in two ways primarily: one, by volunteering to support one or more of the ministries in the church and, two, by leading others to a saving relationship with Jesus Christ.

As I concluded in the first chapter, our spiritual gifts program formalizes principles established by Bob Russell and our eldership when the church first began. We have always insisted that Southeast members be participants in the work of the church and not merely spectators. That hasn't always been the case in churches where I have served in the past. I know you can relate to the following generalized experience I have had at a variety of churches.

At the end of a service the preacher makes an impassioned appeal that the church needs volunteers to (pick one from the following list): a) work in the nursery, b) work in the parking lot usually during the months of February or August, c) clean the restrooms because the family that has been doing it for 25 years transferred their membership to another church, or d) all the above.

Like many Christians I want to do my part and serve Jesus and the church so that we can grow in size and Spirit. But to be honest, none of the above duties sounds very appealing to me. Nevertheless, I am moved to volunteer where the need is greatest and usually find myself stuck in the nursery surrounded by a dozen or so infants crying for no good reason, soiling their diapers unnecessarily, and basically making my life miserable. I love the little ankle biters, but I hate the work and either burn out after six months or look for the first excuse (perhaps enlisting in the French Foreign Legion) to get out of the duty. Now my wife thrives in the nursery and looks forward to her nursery duty. On the other hand, my passion is teaching, and every time I prepare a lesson or I walk into a classroom, my heart beats a little faster.

At Southeast, we have done a good job, I think, matching people's gifts to jobs that appeal to those gifts. Unlike other churches where I have served and burnout is commonplace, it is almost nonexistent at Southeast. Why? I think it is because we have been successful in matching people to the area of service that matches their gifts, temperament, and passion.

Following a Spiritual Gifts class, Les will have each participant complete an "Action/Response Sheet" (Appendix 28), which is the first step in placing a member in a ministry. After providing the requisite information, he schedules an interview with the individual to discuss what they learned in the class and point them in a specific direction with regard to a ministry in which they might want to serve. As far as it went, this was a helpful, though time-consuming process.

However, it became clear to all of us that something more was needed.

I first became aware of this need when I attended the "New Church" convention in San Antonio and listened to various speakers share how formal their process was in matching individuals to specific ministries. Based on this new awareness, we decided to create a new staff position to be responsible for the entire process of spiritual gifts assessment, compiling a comprehensive list of ministry needs/jobs, and then coordinating the interview process to link ministry needs with people who are gifted and available to fill those specific needs. The job description for this position is located at Appendix 29. Basically, the new person will be a job placement counselor for volunteer positions in the church, and we hope to add a "Volunteer Job Placement Center" located prominently in the atrium so people can go directly from the sanctuary to the Volunteer Job Placement Center to inquire about ministry opportunities.

In the area of volunteering, I should mention our annual congregation volunteer recruitment. Like most churches, we give our members an opportunity each year to commit to fulfill their financial responsibilities to God and the church by turning in a commitment card specifying that they will give a certain portion, hopefully a tithe, of their income to God. In 1996, we thought it would be appropriate to challenge our membership to commit not only their money but their time as well. To this end, Bob and Dave preached a series of sermons on discipleship in June, and we gave the campaign widespread publicity.

At the end of the sermon series, we asked our membership to commit to at least one area of ministry for the coming year. About one-third of our congregation made this commitment and either reenrolled in an existing ministry or found a new area of service. This program has become a recurring initiative and provides an annual resurgence of interest in serving as well as providing a fresh group of new volunteers.

For many, serving and evangelizing is a natural by-product of being a Christian. For others the process must be more intentional; they need to be led. This is particularly true in a big church where service opportunities may be less visible and access to those opportunities may be less apparent than in a small church. Likewise, evangelizing the lost can be perceived as someone else's business. The key is providing a logical, straightforward way for new members to get involved and learn how to share their faith with others.

Our formal efforts in the area of personal evangelism grew out of the New Member program. It occurred to us that our ultimate objective was to convert guests to new members and ultimately to "multiplying members" so Southeast could continue to grow in size and Spirit. Unfortunately, **we had a class for all the pieces to the puzzle except personal evangelism.** I suggested that we develop a course called "Share Life," which I thought could be developed as a multiple-session personal evangelism class taught by lay people.

As we were developing this idea, it was suggested that our Associate Minister, Dave Stone, should take on this challenge. His book, *I'd Rather See A Sermon*, focused on the task of evangelizing the lost. So, in 1999 we developed a class called "Building Bridges" that would directly address the first, and most important, item of our mission statement, "To evangelize the lost." The overriding theme was building bridges between your friend and God.

In preparing the course, I studied "Contagious Christianity," "Living Proof," and "Evangelism Explosion." I also attended Willow Creek's evangelism workshop. All of the personal evangelism courses were excellent, but Dave felt a need to develop our own program that would respond more directly to our church culture and values. We place a great emphasis on baptism, for instance, and none of the existing programs adequately dealt with that subject in our opinion.

We conducted our first weekend seminar in November 1999 and over 400 people showed up. Needless to say we were overwhelmed by the response. Too long for a single session, *Building Bridges* was conducted in two sessions, two hours on Friday evening and three hours on Saturday morning. Session 1 focused on "You," the individual. During this session we defined evangelism, provided some positive motivation, and then let the attendees discover their own evangelism style. Session 2 outlined ways to build bridges to your friends. Topics discussed are "Who do you evangelize?" "How do you break down barriers?" and "How to start spiritual conversations." Session 3 focused on the Bridge illustration. Dave taught the basics of the illustration, and then it is demonstrated in a skit. The people in attendance have an opportunity to practice on each other. Our version of the Bridge illustration was included in a tract we had specially prepared for our use since others, while excellent, didn't emphasize the factors most important to us.

After the initial *Building Bridges* class we provided for a quarterly get-together called "Building Bridges Reunion." The purpose of the reunion was to fan the flames of evangelism that had been ignited during the class and to build an ever-increasing core of personal evangelists in the church upon which to build a more effective program. We held the first reunion on a Sunday evening between five and seven o'clock. During that time we shared testimonies, reviewed some material, and basically had a great time together. We had 125 people in attendance and are excited about building a large core of committed evangelists in our church.

Chapter 13
Closing the Back Door

The one who received the seed that fell on rocky places is the man who hears the word and at once receives it with joy. But since he has no root, he lasts only a short time. When trouble or persecution comes because of the word, he quickly falls away.

Matthew 13:20,21

"While countless 'unchurched' people are flocking in the front door of the church, a steady stream of the 'churched' is flowing out the back."[17]

A lady in my ABF class called to tell me that she had transferred her membership to a church in Shelbyville after many years of active membership at Southeast. I was really disappointed. Colleen is bright, studious, and asked intriguing questions in class. I will miss her.

Of course, I wanted to know why she was leaving the church. "It's just grown too big," she confided echoing a comment I hear often. "I need to worship in a more intimate atmosphere," she concluded. Her mom had been ill for several months, and while I had called Colleen a number of times to check up on her mom and while others in the class had visited her mom in the nursing home, I worried that perhaps the class hadn't been as supportive as Colleen needed

125

us to be. That was not the case I was assured. Still, I felt a loss because she was leaving.

This incident, I think, highlights several issues relevant to the assimilation process and reinforces some insightful truths.

ISSUES RELEVANT TO RETENTION

1. First and most importantly, Colleen wasn't really leaving the church. She was just finding another physical location where the body of Christ meets on weekends. I know **we'd all like to think that our church is for everyone, but it isn't.** Southeast is too big for some, including Colleen. On the other side of the coin, I come in contact with people all the time who have moved their membership to Southeast because their former church was too small. That is, the size of the church didn't allow it to provide the requisite programming to meet the needs of the individual.

More often than not the absence of a meaningful children's or youth program is cited for the reason someone left their previous church. But people are also attracted to Southeast because of our support groups, excellence in programming, singles programs, and a host of other activities available because we are a large church with enormous resources.

Our desire is that a person find a place where they can worship and serve God. If that's Southeast, great. If not, we wish them "good luck at their new location." That's the way we feel about people who find a new church home. This reminds me of a Bob Russell joke he tells about a man who had a friend who was relocating his business. He wanted to celebrate his friend's good fortune and ordered some flowers to be sent to the new business location. The next day he visited his friend at the new store and was appalled that the florist had sent a huge arrangement of flowers that said: "Rest in Peace." Irate, he called the florist to complain, but the florist was unsympathetic: "You think you have problems," he said. "Somewhere in this city there is a funeral with an arrangement of flowers that says, 'Good luck at your new location."

2. **We need to know when someone leaves the church.** Most aren't as accommodating as Colleen. When I began to investigate our process of deleting members from our membership roster, I was unpleasantly surprised to find that people were dropped from our membership database, and the ministerial staff never knew they were gone. I discovered that people were being eliminated when: 1) they died, which seemed like a legitimate enough reason; 2) mail was returned without a forwarding address (we placed them in a hold list for two years before deleting them); 3) we received a letter of transfer from another church; and 4) our Telecare ministry was unable to call them. (Telecare is a church ministry that has volunteers call everyone in the church once a year to check on the member and see if they have any special needs or prayer requests.)

This is where smaller churches have a decided advantage over a bigger one. They can take attendance, and I think they should. With this attendance information you have the ability to determine who is not attending regularly. If you then establish an aggressive process of follow-up, you can identify and solve problems that might drive members away from your church, or worse yet, away from the church altogether.

3. **We need to know why someone leaves the church.** Church growth experts have done a lot of research in this area. Writing in the February 19, 1998, edition of *Baptist Today,* Mark Wingfield reports on the work done by Chip Miller and notes that the trek out of the church's back door may take three months or three years, "but the bottom line is that people leave the church because they feel no one in the church is listening to them."

According to Miller "there's always a cluster of painful events that underlie a person's departure, and those events may have happened years before and may or may not involve church events or personalities. . . . However, the end result is that a person leaves a congregation because others failed to notice and act on his hurt."[18]

The availability and accessibility of the ministerial staff is a constant issue in this regard. That is one of the reasons we have a Minister on Call program. We have a staff member on call from 8:00 a.m. to 5:00 p.m. Monday through Friday. This minister carries a radio so he can be contacted readily in the case that the receptionists receive a phone call or someone drops in with a spiritual issue they need to discuss. Our counseling center is also available to see emergencies during the day.

On the other hand, Miller writes,

> when a person's faith is being fed, when he or she is in a group that knows more than just their name, and when they have a sense of being part of the church's vision, the member will likely remain faithful to the church. However, if two or three of these elements begin to unravel and the person begins sitting farther back in the church and missing Sunday School, committee meetings, and special activities, he's probably on his way out.[19]

Why Some People Leave

Why do some people leave the church? Experts tell us that people leave for about eight reasons. (The percentages that follow exceed 100 since most people surveyed cited more than one reason for leaving.)

a. **Physical factors.** The most common reason people leave church is that they move away. Thom Rainer indicated in his research that 70% of the people leave because they move out of the local area.[20] In light of our highly mobile society where the average American moves once every four years, there is little we can do about this factor except expect it to increase.

Given Southeast's phenomenal growth, physical factors other than relocation have certainly played a role. I mean, a

770,000-square-foot building and 9000-seat sanctuary isn't for everyone. I can really sympathize with those people who feel a little intimidated by the huge expanse of our facility. It's a long walk from the parking lot to your seat in the sanctuary. And the crowded parking lot can be a little discouraging as well. Still, these are factors we have to contend with daily when we go to the mall, a basketball game, or the airport. Part of our job is helping people adjust to this new reality.

Due to our enormous growth since 1987, crowding is a problem that has (Praise God!) always plagued Southeast. In our previous 2200 seat sanctuary we held five services on the weekend and crammed over 11,000 people in our facility. Some affectionately called us the "Church of the Sardine." I am delighted that overcrowding is one of our problems. Even in our new, much larger facility, the parking lot is the number one deterrent to future growth. I am confident that once we fix the parking problem there will be another physical challenge awaiting us.

b. **Quality of worship** is a huge factor. As a matter of fact, when asked, most people tell us that the reason they left their former church was that they were not being fed spiritually. Given our dedication to excellence, I do not believe many people leave Southeast because of lack of quality in worship.

c. **No friends.** As previously cited, Win Arn has written that a person needs to make seven friends in their first six months of membership or they will leave the church. I am not sure how this statistic was determined, but it makes sense, and this is the reason we place such a great emphasis on forming relationships in all of our activities.

But this emphasis on relationships is bound to increase in the future. People in our culture are increasingly insulated from each other, and we are losing the sense of community we once enjoyed in our neighborhoods. This point was driven home to me not long after my wife and I purchased our most current home, a condominium. I recall coming home from work one day and using the garage door opener to open the garage door. I watched the door close behind me sealing me in the four walls of my house. I then went in to the den and watched TV, and later, I logged onto my computer and had unfettered access to the information superhighway. I could chat with a ministerial counterpart in South Africa, talk in a chat room with New Age environmentalists, or order a book from Amazon.com. I was stunned when it occurred to me that while I had incredible access to the most distant and remote locations of the world, I had never met my neighbor living not twelve inches from my den. For these reasons, many people coming to church are craving relationships and will leave if they don't feel connected. They want to belong, to be a part of a group, where, like on the TV sitcom *Cheers,* "everybody knows your name."

d. As Chip Miller noted, people leave because **no one listens to them or their needs aren't being met.** This is a common complaint and is more prevalent in a large church. With individuals and families stretched to the breaking point, there are a huge number of people with heartbreaking physical, spiritual, and emotional needs. I talk to them almost every day. In my relatively brief time in the ministry, the number of hurting people I see has astonished me. People struggle with addictions, crushing financial problems, abusive relationships, broken homes, enormous turmoil, and problems that seem insurmountable. Yet despite the severity of the problems, when I counsel with them, all they really seem to want is someone to listen.

e. Some people have **apathy about church generally.** Thom Rainer suggests that 66% of the people who leave, leave for this reason.[21] There's not much we can do about this one except to pray and to make the worship experience as moving and convicting as possible.

f. **Wounded feelings** account for 44% of the people leaving according to Rainer. This is sad but true and seems almost endemic to church life.[22]

g. **Interpersonal conflict** makes up 28% of the people leaving the church.[23]

h. **Feelings of not being needed** is the last reason. Rainer says 14% of the people fall into this category.[24]

4. Once we discover why people leave, **we need to fix problems that drive them away**, if we can. Currently, Southeast's biggest problem is our limited parking, which will support an attendance of about 15,000 each weekend. When we fix the parking problem, another obstacle will take its place. Unfortunately, we can't become smaller to accommodate people like Colleen, but there are still things we can do to make the church seem smaller and friendlier. We work extremely hard trying to be "the smallest big church in America."

SOUTHEAST'S INITIATIVES TO CLOSE THE BACKDOOR

As William Hendricks suggested in the quote at the beginning of this chapter, we do a pretty good job of getting people into our church. We are very intentional about filling our pews and encouraging attendees to get involved in a host of different programs. To be honest, I don't know of any church that does a very good job of finding out who is leaving the church and why they leave. More often than not we don't have a clue when someone leaves the church, and consequently a lot of people enter the church through the front door but later slip out the back door unnoticed. Yet, I think one of the key components of an effective assimilation program is "closing the back door." We've discovered that this is much easier said than done.

To get a better handle on who was leaving Southeast, I found a couple of "statistically gifted" members to do some research. Chuck and Gerry Staebler had provided indispensable assistance when we moved from our old building to our new one. Chuck developed elaborate spreadsheets depicting the location of every piece of equipment in our old building and specifying where each item would be delivered at our new building. We completed the move without one lost item. Now I asked Chuck and Gerry to do essentially the same thing with our membership — make sure we didn't lose any of them. We compiled a list of all people who we had been removed from membership for any reason.

The vast majority moved their membership because they left the local area or we hadn't been able to establish contact with them for two years. So far I am encouraged that we've had "only" about 350 losses of this variety in 1999 . . . that we know about. Our plan was to contact as many people as possible who had transferred their membership to another church and determine why they had left. This is the process we used:

To begin with, we narrowed our study to contact only those people for whom we received letters of transfer from other churches. Everyone was sent a letter from Bob Russell thanking them for being a part of our fellowship here and telling them that we were praying that they would find another church where they could serve at their new location. The letter contained a simple postage and fees paid postcard that asked three questions about their Southeast experience.

1) Why did you leave Southeast? (The recipients were asked to check all that applied.)
   a. Moved from the local area
   b. Church was too big
   c. Church was not user friendly — parking, signage, etc.
   d. Not being fed spiritually
   e. People were not friendly
   f. Disagreed with church on social or doctrinal issues
   g. Offended by another church member
   h. Did not like the worship service.

2) Is there anything we could have done to have prevented you from leaving?
3) Is there anything else you'd like to share with the church's leadership?

We hoped that a significant number of individuals would return the survey and expected that the vast majority of out-of-town addressees would respond that they changed membership due to moving out of the local area. Still, we expected to get some valuable feedback from these people, and we did. For the people who lived in the local area and did not return postcards, we attempted to call them personally to find out why they left and if there was anything we could have done to have kept them from leaving.

Our exit interview process is too new to draw any sweeping conclusions, but we were able to conduct telephone interviews with almost half of the 44 people we determined had left Southeast in 1999 and transferred their membership to another church in the Louisville area. The accompanying table details what we learned. The results are neither surprising nor disappointing. Most encouraging was the revelation that three of the people were still attending Southeast and one individual had moved her membership back to Southeast recently.

Reason Given for Leaving Southeast	Number of responses
New church was closer to home	8
New church was smaller (felt lost at Southeast)	6
People unfriendly or hypocritical	5
Change of marital status, divorced, remarried, or death of a spouse	4
Dissatisfaction with children's program	3
"Big church hassle" — getting from point A to Point B, parking lot, crowds, long walks	3
Influenced by friends to move membership	1

Chart 12: Reasons why people moved membership from Southeast

Two of the people were extremely unhappy with the church, and their grievances ran the gamut from hypocrisy on the part of other members to disagreement with specific subjects discussed in the sermons to feeling like they were not accepted by small groups in which they were involved. Notwithstanding the people who were really turned off, my overall conclusion is that the church is doing a pretty good job of addressing the needs of the congregation but that a big church's size alone creates some structural barriers some people find unacceptable. For instance, one lady had four kids and found the hassle of getting each one of them to their individual classes too stressful.

Even if we didn't reach any profound conclusions, the survey itself has therapeutic value in assuring the congregation that the leadership cares about what they think and, in fact, we did identify some things we can improve upon. As we look to the future, I want to devote even more resources to finding out who is leaving the church and why.

Chapter 14

Applying the Model to Your Church

I pray that you may be active in sharing your faith, so that you will have a full understanding of every good thing we have in Christ.   Philemon 1:6

As I have already suggested, you may use our model, someone else's, or create your own. I recommend you survey the available options and then adapt whatever model you select to your particular church situation. I'm kind of partial to ours, of course, since, unlike most I've seen, ours is the only process that integrates the entire new member process from the time a guest first enters the building until they are fully assimilated.

FIRST THINGS FIRST

Where should you start? Before I prescribe specific actions for specific church situations, I'd like to share seven essential actions necessary for you to implement an effective assimilation program in your church.

1. **Pray.** I know we always say that, but it is really essential that God be invited to lead our efforts. If you don't invite Him aboard at the very beginning, you may produce a wonderful program from the world's point of view, but one

that doesn't accomplish His specific purpose. Twice I conducted a class where only two people showed up. If it had been up to me, I would have canceled the classes as not being worth my time, and the attendees would have agreed. But after I completed the sessions, I was convinced that God met specific pastoral needs of the people who attended and that the needs had nothing to do with the material I planned to present. I say this to reinforce the point that all this is about what *God* wants to accomplish and not what we think the end result should be. If we don't pray, initially and often, we will miss the point. It's just as simple as that.

2. You need to **enlist the support of the church's senior leadership.** I mentioned this in Chapter 4, but it's worth repeating here. The assimilation program must become an integral part of the way the church does business, or it will simply become just another program, a passing fancy, the "Program of the Month," that generates a good deal of enthusiasm, diminishes in importance over time, and then just fades into the background usually to be replaced by the next program that comes along because someone attended a conference or read a new book. Everyone — senior ministers, elders, staff, and lay leaders — needs to be on board.

If you can, get your senior minister and elders to take the initial orientation program. We had our elders and deacons complete our spiritual gifts class before it was offered to the congregation. This was important as it a) got them on board and b) educated them and c) helped promote the program.

3. **Communicate your vision for the program often and in every conceivable manner.** Share your vision one-to-one, in letters, in the church newsletter or newspaper, to any group who'll hold still long enough to listen. Take key leaders to lunch and preach the benefits of an effective assimilation program.

4. **Form a small team of loyal supporters.** We started with assigned deacons. Some didn't have their heart in it, and we let them serve in another area. We added new people as they

expressed an interest. They didn't necessarily have to be deacons, and I was more than just a little pleased that we added seven members to the team who had joined the church in the last year. Don't try to do it all yourself no matter how talented, energetic, or good looking you think you are. You need to equip and empower your laity; start programs and give them away. Then develop another piece to the puzzle, start it, and then give it away.

5. **Start small.** We were blessed because our decision counseling program and spiritual gifts program were up and running, allowing us to concentrate our energies on *Welcome to Southeast!* initially. It's a mistake to try to do it all too quickly. Pick a piece of the process and implement it well. In most cases, you are already doing some parts. Look for an area you are doing well and seek to make that program excellent. Excellence shines. It attracts attention and makes people want to be a part of the program.

6. **Use testimonials.** Tell the success stories that entice others to get involved. This means being alert for stories and pursuing them like a cub reporter who aspires to win a Pulitzer Prize for journalism.

7. **Pray.** I know I've already said that. I'm saying it again. You should begin with prayer, pray during the process, and end with prayer. Pray for the programs and the new members God is going to bring you and the ones He's already brought on board. Also, remember to request the prayers of your lay leadership and volunteers. Periodically we send out Decision Counselor and New Member update letters, and we list specific prayer concerns. The more people you can enlist in your prayer effort the better will be the results.

APPLYING THE MODEL TO YOUR CHURCH

Now let's briefly apply the model to three specific church situations that might apply to your church.

1. **The growing church.** This is the situation we were fortunate to find ourselves in as we moved into our newly completed building and created our program. If this is the case, you should, as we did, devote the majority of your energy to the "Connect" phase. That has to be the first step when you have a large number of people joining your church. For this reason, we fielded our *Welcome to Southeast!* program first. In retrospect, I believe we should have implemented our sponsor program earlier. I also wish we had delayed fielding other programs such as *Discover Life* and *New Life* until we had the other components more fully developed. Even though these were good initiatives, they sapped our organizational energy and distracted the staff and congregation from the more immediate objective of getting our new members connected.

2. **Plateaued church.** If your church is neither growing nor declining, the need is to reinvigorate the existing membership, and that means entering at the growth portion of the model. I believe the imperative is to help current members discover their spiritual gifts and passion. Further, the programming emphasis and the emphasis from the pulpit needs to be on discipleship.

The Spiritual Gifts class can help motivate and enable existing members to get involved. When people come in contact with their spiritual gifts, discover their God-given temperament, and become aware of their passion, they are naturally inspired to serve and get involved. They bring to the church new energy and renewed optimism. Some will find they have a gift of evangelism and start bringing in visitors and new members. Others will discover they are suited to be greeters and enliven the greeters program. Still others will elect to serve in other much needed areas as you seek to have them move into the "Serve" sector of the involvement program. The renewed energy of a spiritual gifts program should help break out of the plateaued rut.

3. **Declining church.** I would recommend the same approach for the declining church except that you need to be

more deliberate and go slower because your resources are less plentiful. Start with one or two programs and do them with excellence. In his book *Turn-Around Churches*, George Barna recommends that churches in decline start by doing a few things well even though the temptation may be to recover by adding to the programs. Churches that offer a broad range of options usually do none well and overburden an already depleted staff and shrinking core of volunteers. He wrote: "Many renewed churches found that people were relieved, rather than disappointed, to have the program roster trimmed severely."[25] So pare away ineffective programs and breathe new life into solid ones.

Chapter 15
How Did We Do?

So neither he who plants nor he who waters is anything, but only God, who makes things grow. 1 Corinthians 3:7

E arly in my initial efforts to create a program, Brett DeYoung, our Administrator of Education, challenged me to develop a method of determining how we were doing. His point was well taken, but the challenge was a daunting one. First, we're a big church, and there are a lot of people to keep up with. We don't take attendance, so how are we to determine who is participating? More to the point, what does "involved" mean? When does a new member qualify as being plugged in? But clearly these were issues that had to be addressed if we were to assess how well we were doing and determine what adjustments were needed to more effectively incorporate new members in our congregation.

For these reasons we conducted a new member survey in the Fall of 1999. This was a temporary measure until we could establish a more reliable enrollment system. I realize the challenges and pitfalls of an enrollment system, and it's not altogether clear that we are willing to collect the information necessary and complete the requisite paperwork to field an accurate assessment of who is involved. That's a subject for a future discussion.

Here's how we conducted our survey. We mailed surveys to 1438 new members who joined between January and October 1999. We had a response rate of 24.7% as 356 were returned. Since I am convinced that the people who are willing to take the initiative to complete a survey are also more likely to take the initiative to get involved in the church, I wanted to force contact with some of the "nonresponders." To that end, 90 of the nonresponders were contacted by phone. Sure enough, 18 percent fewer of the nonresponders were "involved" than were the people who responded to our surveys.

The criteria we used for a new member to be considered "involved" were: They should be a member of a small group or ABF and/or they must volunteer in a ministry at least one hour per month. I'd concede that this is pretty liberal criteria, but we had to start somewhere. In the future we plan to tighten this criteria some.

The results we achieved were pretty encouraging, if not influenced by wishful thinking on behalf of survey participants. Seventy-one percent of those returning cards were involved while 53% of the nonresponders contacted by phone were involved. When the proportional adjustments were made, we concluded that the overall percentage of new members involved was 57%. Within the limitations of the survey, I am pleased with this finding and satisfied that the Southeast assimilation program was helpful in achieving these results. It says to me that, among other things, our new members are aware of the need to be involved in these programs. We concluded a churchwide study about the same time that revealed similar findings.

In talking with other churches' Involvement ministers, we found that their overall involvement rate is between one-third and two-thirds of the congregation. When we look at our congregation as a whole (not just new members) we're probably in the ballpark. We have more than 17,000 members, and I estimate at least a third are involved in some way.

June's volunteer recruitment gathered over 3300 volunteers. Our ABF attendance normally exceeds 2500 while small group participation is about 2700 (granted there is some overlap here in these totals but the aggregate is pretty impressive).

Our new member survey revealed some additional helpful information:

1. **If a new member attended *WTS!* the percentage of involvement rose from 57% to 72.5%.** I was certain there was a positive benefit, and the survey suggested there is, though I'll admit other factors influenced the positive correlation.

2. We asked the respondents to rate our new member program on a scale of 1 (poor) to 10 (excellent). **The overall rating was 8.6** which I think means we met most of their needs pretty well.

3. As an outgrowth of the study, **we collected data on the new member demographics.** The only surprising bit of information was the median age of a new member. I would have expected a median age of 40-45, theorizing that Baby Boomers were coming back to church. In fact, the median age was 37. Since this age falls within the usual criteria for the Baby Buster generation or Gen X, it probably means that we are going to have to begin changing our methods (*not* the message) to provide broader appeal to the peculiarities of this group of Americans. If we are to effectively reach a new generation of believers with the gospel, we must adapt our services and programming to be more appealing to Generation X.

4. **We received numerous positive comments about the church**, e.g., "friendly," "numerous opportunities," "the Word is preached," "the Holy Spirit is in this place," etc. We worked very hard to exalt Christ and preach the Word, so this feedback was particularly welcome.

5. **A sizable number of people who weren't involved indicated they planned to get more involved but they just weren't ready** (12 out of 90 people contacted by phone said they weren't

ready now but did plan to get involved later). This was a big lesson for me since I am not a very patient person. Assimilation takes time, more time than I expected. You really can't push people too much, and as I commented earlier, we've discovered that on average it takes about 18 months for a person to attend before they decide to become a member. It probably takes even longer for the new member to choose to get involved.

Month	New Members	WTS!	Discover Life	Spiritual Gifts	New Life	WWB	Guest Reception	Building Bridges
Jan	328						370	
Feb	189	220					199	
Mar	169	99	12			174	209	
Apr	194	23		75	44		328	
May	264	28	13				319	
June	176	39		75	9		299	
July	169	31					277	
Aug	229	41			18		311	
Sep	149	47	6	51		223	270	
Oct	184	37			2		272	
Nov	190	18		32			236	420
Dec	216						148	
Total	2457	583	31	233	73	397	3338	420

Table 13: How Did We Do in 1999?

The table above details the 1999 participation in each of the programs we offered. Obviously, we were very happy with total number of additions and the number of people who attended our guest reception. As we discussed, neither the *Discover Life* nor the *New Life* classes caught on. We plan to provide greater emphasis on the *Welcome to Southeast!* and raise participation above the current 18% rate since our intent is to make *WTS!* the linchpin of our assimilation program. If we can get 50% of our new members to *WTS!* I am confident that we can make greater strides in getting them to take their next step, whatever that might be. We were extremely pleased with the response to our first *Building Bridges* offering. In the area of Spiritual Gifts and *What We Believe*, we need to ensure that at least 30 percent of our people have an opportunity to take these classes and we have established a goal that we reach this figure by 2004.

In concluding this chapter, I'd like to share a story that I think illustrates the importance of casting a challenging, God-honoring vision for your church. Our goals may seem unattainable to you in your church. I recommend that you not compare your church with ours today. Rather, compare your church to Southeast in 1962 or 1966 or even in the mid-'80s. At that time we were averaging just under 2,000. About the same time we had a Sunday evening service that our youth conducted. They ushered, took up the offering, led the music, and served as greeters. During the sermon time, three teenagers gave brief testimonials about what Southeast meant to them. One young man, Barry Wooley, spoke about his vision for Southeast, and during a staff meeting a couple of years ago our Research Associate Rusty Russell played an audio tape of Barry's testimonial. Barry shared how much Southeast had meant to him, and then he talked about the Southeast of the future. He said he could see a time when 10,000 people came to the church on a weekend. There was a pause, and as we listened to the tape, we heard someone laugh, and then another laughed, and soon seemingly the entire congregation was laughing at the thought that Southeast might grow in a few short years to a worship attendance of 10,000. But, of course, we now know that that is precisely what happened. Rusty summed up his feeling about the tape he had just shared by saying that he could see a Southeast where 100,000 people came to church on a weekend, and nobody laughed.

I pray that out of his glorious riches he may strengthen you with power through his Spirit in your inner being, so that Christ may dwell in your hearts through faith. And I pray that you, being rooted and established in love, may have power, together with all the saints, to grasp how wide and long and high and deep is the love of Christ, and to know this love that surpasses knowledge—that you may be filled to the measure of all the fullness of God.

Now to him who is able to do immeasurably more than all we ask or imagine, according to his power that is at work within us, to him be glory in the church and in Christ Jesus throughout all generations, for ever and ever! Amen.

Ephesians 3:16-21

Chapter 16

The Future Ain't
What It Used to Be

Standing at the beginning of a new millennium, it is more than a little unnerving trying to keep up with the rapid-fire changes that are having a dramatic impact on our personal lives and on the church. While we may disagree on the extent of these changes, there is little disagreement that the church faces challenges today unprecedented in our lifetime, perhaps unprecedented in the history of the church. Not since the 15th century, when Martin Luther launched the Protestant Reformation and Gutenberg provided the technology for individual access to the Word of God, have both the media and the message been so radically affected.

It is my personal opinion, and that of others more knowledgeable than I, that we are at a hinge point of history. Leith Anderson used that term in an article which appeared in *Bibliotheca Sacra*.[26] He compared our hinge point with the time of Christ, the fall of the Roman Empire, the Renaissance, the Reformation, and the Industrial Revolution. When viewed from our perspective in history, we can look back and say that nothing, especially the church, was the same after the hinge was opened. In 1993 Peter Drucker, one of the most astute social observers of our time, voiced a similar thought when he said:

> Every few hundred years in Western history there occurs a sharp transformation. Within a few short decades, society rearranges itself — its worldview; its basic values; its social and political structure; its arts, its key institutions. Fifty years later, there is a new world. And the people born then cannot even imagine the world in which their grandparents lived and into which their own parents were born. We are currently living through just such a transformation[27]

If these commentators are correct, the changes we will experience will be so sweeping that we will not be able to recognize the church in 25 years. In this final chapter I will briefly and certainly simplistically characterize the forces shaping our culture today and in the future and then suggest how these changes may affect the new member assimilation process.

CHANGES ON THE HORIZON

The changes we are seeing result from the confluence of three huge changes all coming together at one moment in time. Those changes are: 1) the Information Revolution; 2) a significant, but not unprecedented, generational change, the so-called Generation Xers; and most importantly 3) the beginning of our postmodern culture. Let me briefly discuss each one of these movements.

The Information Age

In their book *The Third Wave,* Alvin and Heidi Toffler describe civilization's major technological revolutions as waves breaking over the beach. As each wave breaks upon the shore, there is considerable turmoil and commotion that is replaced by calm as the waters recede only to be replaced by another crashing wave. They suggested that in the history of civilization there have been three waves, or revolutions. **The first wave was the Agricultural Revolution** when we domesticated animals and began to produce enough crops to support more than a family unit. This development enabled cities to be formed. Not too surprisingly, the key to power was the land you possessed and the most important tools were farm implements.

The second wave occurred during the 17th to 19th centuries depending on the region of the world. **This was the Industrial Revolution**, which brought us mass production and intense urbanization. Our culture was profoundly affected by this wave in every aspect of our lives. The key to power became less the territory you possessed than it did the industrial capability you were able to generate. The main tool was the gas driven engine.

This wave gave way to the current Information Revolution, which is also having a dramatic influence on our society. Of course, the main tool now is the computer, and knowledge is the key to power. Given the ready and almost universal access to information provided by computers and the Internet, the emphasis is now less on mass and more on demassification; less on bureaucratic, hierarchical systems and more on networking and interactive systems. The Third Wave is responsible for accelerating cycles of styles, trends, ideas, and inventions to mind-boggling speeds.

Generation X

The second major force shaping our culture today is generational. Intergenerational conflict is nothing new. Down through history, the older generation has always complained that the next one is going to the dogs. I read the following quote in a church bulletin, so it has to be true. "Our earth is degenerate in these latter days. Bribery and corruption are common. Children no longer obey their parents. Every man wants to write a book. [Ouch. That hurts!] The end of the world is evidently approaching." This quote was allegedly inscribed on a stone slab in Assyria and dates back to 2800 B.C.

Billy Graham has said that "Christianity is one generation away from extinction." That realilty adds to the imperative to reach out to the generation that will replace Baby Boomers in the church. That is the so called "Generation X" or "Gen Xers." Generation X, coming as it is in proximity to other dramatic changes, is particularly worrisome. Let me say quickly however, I do not subscribe to the notion that this generation is inherently bad, lazy, stupid, or whatever pejorative descriptions you may have heard. At the same time, their values are significantly different from their Baby Boomer parents. In their book, *The Fourth Turning*, Strauss and Howe present a fascinating, historical account of generational theory that is most illuminating.

Generation Xers or Baby Busters, were born basically between 1962 and 1981 and are children of the Baby Boom generation born just after World War II. Experts disagree on the exact dates but we'll use 1943–1961 as the birth year for the Boomers. As a Boomer myself, I'm not very proud of what we did to the generation of our children. These children are often the product of divorce, broken homes, a huge national debt, a faulty educational system, a government that fails to live up to its promises, and a society apparently bereft of common morality. For these reasons, Gen Xers possess a troubling list of characteristics, at least from a Boomer's point of view. **As a sweeping generalization, Busters tend to be slow to commitment, distrustful of institutions, indifferent to authority, and self-oriented.** Whereas their workaholic parents work for work's sake, frequently at the expense of the family, Gen Xers work to play and are often not particularly ambitious. They thrill at living on the edge and place a high value on relationships. I hope you're not content with this brief generalization and will read more on the subject, perhaps George Barna's book, *Generation Next*.

Postmodernism

The final force affecting our culture is a philosophy or worldview called postmodernism. This is not nearly as arcane as it sounds, but before we define the term, some background is in order. You may wish to refer to the accompanying diagram. The modern world had its origin in the 17th-century Enlightenment and to a lesser degree in the Renaissance before that. The premodern world, before the scientific revolution, was mystical and superstitious because so little was known about the world around us.

Premodern			Modern Era				Postmodern
1650	1700	1750	1800	1850	1900	1950	2000
Enlightenment			French Revolution				Berlin Wall Down

Premodern	Modern	Postmodern
I believe therefore I am	I think therefore I am	I am
Truth found in God	Truth from Science	No absolute truth
Theocracy	Knowledge	Experience
Belief	Thinking	Feelings
Theism	Deism/Humanism	Existentialism
Catholicism	Protestantism	Pantheism/Syncretism
Day to day	Utopian	Pessimistic
Divine Right of Kings	Democracy	Transnational
Extended family	Nuclear family	No family?
Land a value	Wealth a value	Environment a value
Isolation	Uniformity	Diversity
Superstition	Linear Thinking	Matrix
Local Autonomy	Centralized control	Networking
Local communities	Nationalism	Tribalism, globalism

Chart 14: Timeline of postmodernism

Perhaps it was Descartes who gave the new worldview its identifying motto when he said, "I think, therefore I am." With thinkers like Descartes and Newton and the scientific age, the worldview became decidedly more rational and optimistic than the premodern world it replaced. Now it seemed that mankind had the potential to improve his condition significantly. Humanism began, and the utopian tendencies of communism had their origin in the modern worldview. This worldview didn't reject God exactly, but Theism was replaced to a certain extent by Deism, and the church began to explain God rationally. Apologetics were the way we convinced others that they needed God.

It is impossible to define with any precision where these worldviews begin or end, but I like to think of modernism beginning with the French Revolution and ending with the collapse of the Berlin Wall. The only problem with modernism/humanism is that it doesn't work, as Christians know, because of sin and our fallen nature. Thus about the middle part of the 20th century, many became disenchanted with modernism. **Philosophically, we began to reject modernism and in its place substitute a decidedly pessimistic worldview that focuses on feelings and experience and rejects the notion that there is one, absolute truth.** This is the most troublesome aspect of postmodernism in my opinion because it denies the very substance of what Christianity has to offer, i.e., the absolute truth that God has a plan of salvation for all of mankind that is only accessible through His Son Jesus Christ and that the substance of that plan is revealed only in the Bible.

So how does the church exist in this culture? First, I submit that **we must commit ourselves to change everything we can except the message of the gospel.** As George Barna said in the quote cited previously, we are already way behind the secular cycle of change. Given the rapidity with which our culture is reinventing itself (perhaps as often as every 3-5 years), we will allow the church to become irrelevant if we sit on our hands. Whether you read secular experts such as Tom Peters or Christian gurus such as Leith Anderson, Lyle Schaller, and Carl George, the church is going to have to make profound changes in the way we do business or we run the risk of becoming increasingly marginalized and irrelevant to the culture around us.

Second, **our outreach is going to have to become less rational and more relational.** I like the way Carl George said it at the Leadership Network Conference in San Antonio, Texas, in the Fall of 1999. "We need to think livingroom, not classroom." Because Boomers were a product of the modern world, we sought to convince others of the rational superiority of Christianity, and we spent lots of time teaching. Postmoderns of all stripes, Gen X, Boomers, Millennials, etc. are not as receptive to being taught or convinced as they are to being won over through the cultivation of a relationship. It was a profound revelation to me when it occurred to me that this was precisely Christ's approach. He argued with the Pharisees to a certain extent, and He taught a lot. But His approach to people was primarily relational. So it will be in the postmodern world, and this is an exciting opportunity for the church if we can step out of our comfort zone and become more relational. How do we do that? I haven't a clue, but we have commissioned a study group at Southeast to answer that very question.

Third, because many are turned off by "the church" and all its trappings, I suspect that **we will move more and more of our programming off campus.** Our current paradigm is to attract the unchurched and seekers to the sanctuary, dazzle them with a wonderful worship experience, and convict them by superb, rational/modern worldview sermons, encourage them to join the church and get involved in a small group.

It is quite possible that in the future the process will follow a reverse process. A seeker is invited into the home of a believer or to some neutral location to develop a relationship and discuss issues of mutual interest. Over time, a much longer time than with a Boomer, a relationship might develop and the issues evolve into more deeply spiritual matters leading to the person accepting Jesus as Lord and Savior. At some point in the process, the individual may begin to go to church. I am reminded of the scripture in Acts 2:46-47, "Every day they continued to meet together in the temple courts. They broke bread in their homes and ate together with glad and sincere hearts, praising God and enjoying the favor of all the people. And the Lord added to their number daily those who were being saved."

Fourth, I also think **we need to more consciously reach out to other cultures.** It has been said that the most segregated hour in America is 11:00 on Sunday morning. The church has, actually, quite understandably, reached out primarily to people who are like themselves. Not only are minority groups and other ethnic groups increasing in number, but with their inclination to embrace diversity, Gen Xers and Millennials will be judging the church by how heterogeneous it is.

Fifth, **the church must embrace technology.** I have heard that Francis Schaffer once said that the church specializes in being behind the times. Most of us are still stuck on the printed word when our culture has moved quickly into television first and now the computer monitor and the Internet. If we are to be relevant to a new culture and present the eternal message of salvation in Jesus Christ in a manner so people will listen, we must make full use of all available technological systems.

Sixth, **we will need to continue to provide for involvement opportunities within the four walls of the church.** But there will be more variations and options available to be assimilated, and one of those options will be an increase in the number of service opportunities available. More and more, I see our service being performed in the community. Our local outreach staff tells me that a large number of people participating in our local outreach are not members, but prospects and regular attenders who want to serve. To create more service opportunities, I think the church will begin its own nonprofit parachurch organizations and seek more opportunities to partner with other parachurch organizations.

People will enter the Southeast model at multiple locations in the process I have described in this book. We are already seeing people wait years to join the church, yet they are still actively involved. If we are reading the postmodern world correctly, the model is far too linear to be of much use. Since Gen Xers and others are wired to think more in a matrix than linear pattern, the next-step mode will be less compelling. Since they rely more on experience and feeling, connection opportunities need to become even more relational and less structured.

Finally, **we need to change our evangelism paradigm.** When we go on "cross-cultural" mission trips overseas, we prepare ourselves to understand the culture of the locals, we learn to speak their language as best we can, we take shots to immunize our bodies against disease, we pack the appropriate clothing, and we take Bibles and other materials written in the native language. I would submit that that is precisely what we must do today when we leave the church and go into our workplace or our neighborhood. The majority of people we encounter know nothing of the Bible and won't accept it as truth anyway. If we are to be effective in communicating the gospel message, we're going to have to learn how to speak their language and we're going to have to learn how to get their attention. As Stanley Grenz wrote in *A Primer on Postmodernism*:

> The Gospel of Jesus Christ has gone forth in every era with power to convert human hearts. Today that gospel is the answer to the longings of the postmodern generation. Our task as Christ's disciples is to embody and articulate the never-changing good news of available salvation in a manner that the emerging generation can understand. Only then can we become the vehicles of the Holy Spirit in bringing them to experience the same life-changing encounter with the triune God from whom our entire lives derive their meaning.[28]

I love the way Brad Cecil sums up his feelings about doing church in the new millennium. In an interview in the Winter issue of *Next* magazine he responded to the question, "How do you respond to those who say that postmodernity poses a threat to Christianity?" by saying:

While there are definitely challenges, I feel it is just a reminder that we are always missionaries. We have visited the mission field and it is us! We have to think again as missionaries, re-think what it means to be the Body of Christ in this new culture, and view postmodern culture as we would any other foreign culture.[29]

What does the future hold for your church? God only knows. Certainly when I responded to the invitation on July 1, 1962, and joined 52 others to begin Southeast Christian Church, I never dreamed God would grow our church to be one of the largest in the nation. Yet that is precisely what He has done. I believe that much of our growth can be attributed to an effective assimilation program that is based on some fundamental, sound principles of involvement we have discussed. I pray that our new member assimilation process may be of use to you and your church and that perhaps in the near future you'll have some prescient teenager give you a vision of a church where 10,000 come to worship.

Endnotes

1. Thom Rainer, *High Expectations* (Nashville: Broadman & Holman, 1999), p. 67.
2. *USA Today* (April 1, 1999), p. 1.
3. *Los Angeles Times* (June 17, 1999), p. 1.
4. Jim Collins, *Built to Last* (New York: Harper Business, 1997), p. 93.
5. Thomas Peters and Robert Waterman, *In Search of Excellence* (New York: Warner Books, 1982), p. 318.
6. Tom Peters, *Thriving on Chaos* (London: Pan Books, 1989) p. 45.
7. William Hendricks, *Exit Interviews* (Chicago: Moody Press, 1993), p. 29.
8. *Reformed Worship* (March 1996), pp. 11-13.
9. Roy M. Oswald and Speed B. Leas,*The Inviting Church* (**City??**: Alban Institute, 1987), p. 27.
10. W. Charles Arn, "Evangelism or Disciple Making," *Church Growth State of the Art,* Ed. C. Peter Wagner (Wheaton, IL: Tyndale, 1986), pp. 64-65.
11. George Barna, *The Second Coming of the Church* (Nashville: Word, 1998), p. 8.
12. Hendricks, "Prepare God's People for Works of Service,"*Exit Interviews,* p. 19.
13. Rainer, *High Expectations,* p. 45.
14. Ibid., p. 23.
15. Ibid., p. 104.
16. Ibid., p. 23.
17. Hendricks, "Countless Unchurched,"*Exit Interviews*, jacket cover.
18. Mark Wingfield, "Current Thoughts and Trends,"*Baptist Today* (June 1998), p. 22.
19. Ibid.
20. Rainer, *High Expectations,* p. 155.
21. Ibid, p. 156.
22. Ibid.
23. Ibid.
24. Ibid.
25. George Barna, *Turn-Around Churches* (Ventura, CA: Regal Books, 1993), p. 79.

26. Leith Anderson, "The Church at History's Hinge," *Bibliotheca Sacra* (Jan-Mar 1994), pp. 3-10.
27. Peter Drucker, *Post-capitalistic Society* (New York: Harpers Business, 1994), p. 5.
28. Stanley Grenz, *A Primer on Post Modernism* (Grand Rapids: Eerdmans, 1996), p. 174.
29. Brad Cecil, *Next*, Leadership Network, Vol. 6 (January–March 2000), p. 3.

Bibliography

Barna, George. *Turn-Around Churches*. Ventura, CA: Regal Books, 1993.

_____. *The Second Coming of the Church*. Nashville: Word, 1998.

Hendricks, William D. *Exit Interviews*. Chicago: Moody Press, 1993.

Oswald, Roy, and Speed Leas. *The Inviting Church*. New York: The Alban Institute, 1897.

Rainer, Thom, *High Expectations*. Nashville: Broadman & Holman, 1999.

Schaller, Lyle E. *Assimilating New Members*. Ed. by Lyle E. Schaller. Creative Leadership Series. Nashville: Abingdon, 1978.

Woods, C. Jeff. *Congregational MegaTrends*. New York: The Alban Institute, 1996.

Warren, Rick. *The Purpose Driven Church*. Grand Rapids: Zondervan, 1995.

Appendixes

1 Invitation to WTS!

2 Bulletin Tear-off

3 Letter, person calling for information about church

4 Letter, first time visitor

5 Letter, Southeast beliefs

6 Letter, interested in baptism

7 Letter, interested in baptism unable to reach by phone

8 Letter, inquiry about baptism

9 Letter, inquiry about baptizing a child

10 Letter, to person attending guest reception

11 Letter, person returning feedback questionnaire

12 Prayer before Calling

13 Phone Call Script, First Time Guest

14 Phone Call Script, Interested in Membership Calls

15 Phone Call Script, Weekend Respondents Calls

16 Spotlight

17 Application to be a decision counselor

18 Next step card

19 Sponsor program materials

20 Letter to teachers about sponsor program

21 Lesson Plan for Discipleship and Sponsor Program

22 WTS! brochure

23 Copy of slides used in Welcome to Southeast!

24 WTS! notetaker

25 Basic Bible lessons

26 Discover Life notetaker

27 New Life notetaker

28 Action/Response sheet

29 Job description for Involvement Ministry Assistant

30 Job Description for Involvement Secretary

31 Decision Counseling Sheet

These appendixes may be found at *www.collegepress.com* and are available for your use under copyright conditions delineated on pages 8 and 44 of this book.